The College of Law
of England and Wales

LIBRARY SERVICES

INTN
Tre
Std

Understanding Trade Law

Understanding Trade Law

Michael J. Trebilcock

Professor of Law and Economics, Faculty of Law, University of Toronto, Canada

Edward Elgar

Cheltenham, UK • Northampton, MA, USA

Published by
Edward Elgar Publishing Limited
The Lypiatts
15 Lansdown Road
Cheltenham
Glos GL50 2JA
UK

Edward Elgar Publishing, Inc.
William Pratt House
9 Dewey Court
Northampton
Massachusetts 01060
USA

A catalogue record for this book
is available from the British Library

Library of Congress Control Number: 2011925732

ISBN 978 0 85793 145 0 (cased)
ISBN 978 0 85793 149 8 (paperback)

Typeset by Servis Filmsetting Ltd, Stockport, Cheshire
Printed and bound by MPG Books Group, UK

Contents

v

Preface

This introductory book on international trade law (principally GATT/WTO law) builds on a 25-year-long involvement in the field. Over this period I have taught an introductory trade law course at the University of Toronto Faculty of Law and as a visitor at New York University Law School, Yale Law School, the University of Virginia Law School, and Tsinghua Law School (Beijing) – sometimes with co-teachers including my former student, former colleague, and co-author Robert Howse (now at NYU Law School), Donald Macdonald, former Minister of Finance for Canada, and Dr. Sylvia Ostry, former Senior Trade Negotiator for Canada. I have also authored or co-authored numerous scholarly articles on issues in international trade law and a major treatise, with Robert Howse, *The Regulation of International Trade* (London: Routledge, 3rd edition, 2005), now in the course of being revised in its fourth edition. My experience as a teacher, author, occasional policy advisor or expert witness, and media commentator in the international trade field has underscored to me the need for a short, straightforward account of the basic structure and principles of international trade law that is widely accessible to beginning students and non-specialist scholars and policy advisors. Our treatise (which runs to 600 pages) presupposes a need or desire to invest in acquiring a sophisticated understanding of the field that is beyond what this broader readership requires. My hope in writing this book is that this broader readership, with a limited investment of time and intellectual effort, can acquire a basic understanding of the field, while recognizing that acquiring a more sophisticated understanding of the complexities of the field will require much larger investments of time and effort. In my view, the basic elements of international trade law are no more arcane or inaccessible than any other area of law.

Throughout the book, I have kept citations to relevant case law and scholarly literature to a minimum, while nevertheless providing references to basic sources that readers can pursue if they wish.

In writing this book, I have had the benefit of helpful comments on earlier drafts from anonymous reviewers and my colleague, Andrew Green, who specializes in the field, which have substantially improved the final version and for which I am greatly indebted. I am also indebted to legions of students who have challenged me constantly to render the field of international trade law both accessible and interesting to them. Finally, I am also extremely grateful to my assistant, Nadia Gulezko, for her endless patience and meticulousness in correcting numerous drafts of the manuscript.

1. Setting the context

I. CLASSICAL FREE TRADE THEORY

Members of different societies have traded with each other since the beginning of recorded history.[1] However, one of the first efforts to articulate a rigorous intellectual basis for the economic benefits of facilitating trade between members of different societies was made by Adam Smith. In *The Wealth of Nations*, published in 1776, Adam Smith argued that the gains that could be realized from specialization in domestic economic activity could readily be extended to international economic activity.[2]

> The tailor does not attempt to make his own shoes, but buys them off the shoemaker. The shoemaker does not attempt to make his own clothes, but employs a tailor... What is prudence in the conduct of every private family, can scarcely be folly in that of a great kingdom. If a foreign country can supply us with a commodity cheaper than we ourselves can make it, better buy it off them with some part of the produce of our own industry, employed in a way in which we have some advantage.[3]

Smith's Theory of Absolute Advantage essentially stated that countries should export those products which they can produce more efficiently than other countries and import those products which they cannot. For example, if countries with tropical climates can produce bananas or pineapples more cheaply than countries with temperate climates, the latter should purchase these products from

---

[1]   See William J. Bernstein, *A Splendid Exchange: How Trade Shaped the World* (New York: Atlantic Monthly Press, 2008).
[2]   For a comprehensive account of the intellectual history of free trade theory, see Douglas A. Irwin, *Against the Tide: An Intellectual History of Free Trade* (Princeton, NJ: Princeton University Press, 1996).
[3]   Adam Smith, *The Wealth of Nations* (1776) (reprinted New York: Modern Library Edition, 1937) at 424.

the former. Conversely, if countries with industrialized economies can produce hydro-electric plants or communications systems more efficiently than countries that enjoy a cost advantage in producing tropical fruit, the latter should buy these products from the former. In Smith's view, international trade is merely a means by which to broaden the division of labour by expanding the size of the market. It is important to note that according to Smith's theory, *unilateral* trade liberalization would be an advantageous policy for a country to pursue. Even if other countries did not liberalize their trade policy, a country which did liberalize its trade policy could realize economic gains by importing products made more efficiently by foreigners.

It is equally easy to appreciate the force of this argument for free trade within nation states. For example, in a large federal state like the U.S., Michigan specializes in producing automobiles (*inter alia*), Florida citrus fruits and tourism, Texas oil and beef, and California wine and high-technology products. If each state of the U.S. were to have attempted to become self-sufficient in these and all its other needs, the U.S. would today be immeasurably poorer.

A key question raised by Smith's Theory of Absolute Advantage is what relevance international trade has to a country that has no absolute advantage, that is, a country which cannot produce any product more efficiently than its trading partners. This question was addressed by David Ricardo's Theory of Comparative Advantage, set out in his book *The Principles of Political Economy*, published in 1817. Ricardo famously postulated the following scenario: Portugal can produce a given quantity of wine with 80 units of labour, and a given quantity of cloth with 90 units of labour. England can produce the same quantity of wine with 120 units of labour, and the same quantity of cloth with 100 units of labour. Thus, Portugal enjoys an absolute advantage over England in both wine and cloth. Ricardo argued that trade between the two countries was still mutually advantageous. England is able to export cloth which took 100 units of labour to produce in exchange for wine which it would have required 120 units of labour to produce. Similarly, Portugal, by exporting wine which it took 80 units of labour to produce, gains cloth which would have taken 90 units of labour to produce. Both countries are rendered better off through trade. Another way of understanding the same intuition is to imagine the following simple domestic example.[4] Suppose a lawyer is not only more efficient in the provision of legal services than her secretary, but is also a more efficient secretary. It takes her secretary twice as long to type a document as it would if the lawyer typed it herself. Suppose, more specifically, that it takes the lawyer's secretary two hours to type a document that the lawyer could type in one hour, and that the secretary's hourly wage is $20, and that the lawyer's hourly rate to clients is $200. It would pay the lawyer to hire the secretary and pay her $40 to type the document in two hours while the lawyer is able to sell for $200 the hour of her time that would otherwise have been committed to typing the document. In other words, both the lawyer and the secretary gain from this exchange.

Ricardo's insight was that the crucial question is the relative or comparative advantage of one country vis-à-vis another in producing a product. In other words, the issue is not whether Portugal can produce both wine and cloth more efficiently than Britain, but rather Portugal's relative efficiency in producing cloth versus producing wine compared to Britain's relative efficiency in producing the same goods. In an international trade context, this generalizes to the proposition that a country should specialize in producing and exporting goods in which its comparative advantage is greatest, or comparative disadvantage is smallest, and should import goods in which its comparative disadvantage is greatest.

Although Ricardo's theory still constitutes the basis of conventional international trade theory, it has been refined by subsequent analysis. One deficiency in Ricardo's theory is that it assumes that countries will specialize completely in those products in which they have a comparative advantage, without taking into account the possibility of decreasing returns to scale. Hecksher and Ohlin's Factor Proportions Hypothesis recognized that most products were a function of multiple factors of production (in the case of wine, land and labour), and that combining factors of production at ever-increasing levels of output did not necessarily lead to increasing production in constant proportions. For example, bringing more land into the production of wine may result in utilizing less productive land which requires more intensive use of labour. In recognition of these

---

[4] Adapted from P. Samuelson and A. Scott, *Economics* (Toronto: McGraw-Hill, 1980) at 807.

considerations, the Factor Proportions Hypothesis states that countries will tend to specialize in producing foods that use their abun-
dant factors of production more intensively, and will import goods
that use their scarce factors more intensively.

The Factor Proportions Hypothesis does not, however, provide
an adequate explanation of manufacturing activities in advanced
industrialized economies. Casual observation suggests that firms
in different countries often specialize in different segments of the
same or closely related product markets, simultaneously importing
and exporting products in these sectors. The Product Cycle Theory,
developed by Raymond Vernon, incorporates the idea that products
undergo a variety of stages in their life cycle, and firms in different
countries will specialize in their manufacture depending upon the
particular stage the product is in.[5] Highly developed economies will
tend to specialize in the manufacture of products in the early stages of
development, where financial capital, specialized human capital and
innovation are at a premium. In the later stages of the product cycle,
as production technology becomes standardized, it is adopted by producers in other countries, typically countries with lower labour costs.
At this point in the product cycle, comparative advantage shifts to
these countries. Moreover, as is evident in the increasingly globalized
production chains for many products (e.g., automobiles, computers),
different countries may have a comparative advantage in different
stages of the production process for given products.

II.   QUALIFICATIONS TO THE CASE FOR FREE TRADE

A.   Reciprocity

The development of the current international trade regime has been
animated by the classical theory set out above. However, a great
deal of the debate in international trade law today centers around
the extent to which international trade law should permit deviations
from classical theory.

A major qualification to the case for free trade is the concept of

---

[5]   See Raymond Vernon, "International Investment and International
Trade in the Product Cycle," (1966) 80:2 *Quarterly Journal of Economics* 190.

reciprocity. Recall that classical trade theory views unilateral trade liberalization as advantageous for the liberalizing country. From this perspective, the emphasis placed on reciprocity in trade liberalization commitments in the General Agreement on Tariffs and Trade (GATT) may seem anomalous.[6] However, it is clearly better for the liberalizing country if its trading partners also liberalize, since the first country will realize additional benefits on the export side in addition to the benefits on the import side. One strategy might be for the first country to refuse to remove any of its existing trade restrictions on imports unless its trading partners agree to do the same. This may result in a classic Prisoner's Dilemma game, whereby trading partners who recognize that it is in the first country's interests to liberalize no matter what the trading partners do will withhold concessions in the hopes of gaining the benefits of the first country's liberalization for free. The dominant strategy becomes protectionism, and such individually rational action leads to an inefficient collective outcome of restrictive trade policies.[7] Trade agreements incorporating reciprocal tariff reductions thus offer governments a means of escape from a Prisoner's Dilemma.[8]

Reciprocity is also important from a political economy standpoint. Certain domestic producer interests may oppose any governmental effort to liberalize trade policy on the import side if they are likely to be uncompetitive with foreign producers in the absence of tariffs. If it is to be politically tenable for a government to engage in such liberalization, it will likely need concessions from its trading partners on the export side in order to enlist the countervailing political support of export-oriented producer interests. According to Bagwell and Staiger, one of the main functions of trade agreements is that they represent credible commitments by governments that they will not protect certain industries.[9] In summary, while the

---

[6]   Kyle Bagwell and Robert W. Staiger, *The Economics of the World Trading System* (Cambridge, MA: MIT Press, 2002) at 7.

[7]   Bernard M. Hoekman and Michel M. Kostecki, *The Political Economy of the World Trading System: The WTO and Beyond* (New York: Oxford University Press, 2001, 2nd edn.) at 109.

[8]   Bagwell and Staiger, *supra* note 6 at 3.

[9]   Bagwell and Staiger, *supra* note 6 at 4; see also Douglas A. Irwin, Petros C. Mavroidis, and Alan O. Sykes, *The Genesis of the GATT* (New York: Cambridge University Press, 2008), Chapter 3, for a discussion of economic and political rationales for trade agreements.

concept of reciprocity plays a marginal role in classical trade theory, it is nonetheless crucial to an understanding of the institutional arrangements that govern international trade.

B. The Optimal Tariff

A second qualification to the case for free trade is the concept of the so-called Optimal Tariff. On this theory, countries that account for a large proportion of international demand for a particular good may exercise monopsony power by imposing a tariff which effectively forces exporters from other countries to reduce the price of their products and absorb the tariff. Consumers pay the same price for the good as before, and the government gains revenue from the tariff. While arguably maximizing national welfare, these policies are likely to reduce global welfare and, if replicated by foreign countries, are also likely to reduce national welfare. Bagwell and Staiger argue that the centrality of principles of reciprocity and non-discrimination in the GATT can in part be explained as an attempt by countries (particularly larger countries) to escape from a terms-of-trade driven (non-cooperative) Prisoner's Dilemma where each country, acting unilaterally, has incentives to adopt trade policies (e.g., tariffs on imports, taxes on exports) that externalize a high proportion of the costs of its trade policies onto foreigners. "Beggar-thy-neighbour" trade policies adopted by many countries during the Great Depression are often viewed as exemplifying this danger.

C. Infant Industries

A third qualification relates to infant industries.[10] In the early stages of a country's economic development, a case may be made that import restrictions are justified in order to permit domestic industry to develop by selling to a protected domestic market. Ideally, such protection is temporary and the infant industry eventually develops the scale and sophistication required to compete not only in a liberalized domestic market but also in international export markets. A case in point is the "special and differential status" accorded to less-developed countries (LDCs) under the GATT, which permits

---

[10]   See Irwin, *supra* note 2, Chapter 8.

them to protect domestic industries and engage in import substitution trade policies to some extent. A variant of the infant industry argument is Strategic Trade Theory, which argues that governments can assist domestic firms in establishing strategically dominant preemptive positions in industries where economies of scale imply that there is room for only a limited number of firms in international markets (e.g., large jet airplane manufacturers), in part by maintaining entry barriers to potential foreign competitors or subsidizing domestic firms.[11]

However, the case for government-led protection and/or promotion of domestic industries may be critiqued on a number of grounds, chiefly: (i) private capital markets may be better equipped than governments to identify the long-term growth potential, if any, for an infant industry, and should thus be relied on rather than government to "pick winners"; and (ii) the vulnerability of governments to capture by rent-seeking special interests with regard to the decision to promote and sustain an infant industry through trade-restrictive policies.[12] Nevertheless, according to some commentators, a number of the high-performing East Asian economies have deployed infant-industry protection policies or strategic trade theory successfully; other developing countries much less successfully. It is also true that many currently developed countries early in their development adopted extensive infant-industry protection policies (e.g., the U.S., Canada, Germany).

D. Revenue Raising

A fourth qualification to the case for free trade relates to the revenue-raising potential of customs duties. In industrialized countries, personal, consumption, and business taxes constitute the vast majority of government revenue. However, in less developed countries with weak internal taxation systems, import and export duties are often an important source of government revenue and may be difficult to replace in the short term.

---

[11] See Paul R. Krugman (ed.), *Strategic Trade Policy and the New International Economics* (Cambridge, MA: MIT Press, 1986).

[12] See Robert E. Baldwin, "The Case Against Infant Industry Protection," (1969) 77:3 *Journal of Political Economy*, 295–305.

E. National Security

A final qualification to the case for free trade relates to national security considerations. These may arise on both the import and the export sides. With respect to imports, it is often argued that there may sometimes be a case for trade restrictions in order to protect domestic industries which, even though not internationally competitive, may be required in the event of war or other international disruptions (e.g, domestic steel or coastal shipping industries). On the export side, national security considerations have sometimes been invoked to restrict exports of strategically sensitive products or military materiel to "unfriendly" foreign countries. More generally, trade agreements are often designed to serve broader foreign policy objectives, for example greater economic integration may enhance global or regional peace and reduce the potential for military conflicts by raising the costs of such conflicts. This was clearly a major rationale for the emergence of the European Community and also seems to have been part of the motivation for the GATT.

F. Adjustment Costs

A further qualification to the case for free trade relates to the adjustment costs that firms, workers, and communities may face with the abrupt forms of trade liberalization and argue for gradual implementation of such policies.

G. Health, Safety and Environmental Concerns

Where imports threaten the health, safety and environmental conditions of citizens in importing countries, trade restrictions may be justified to minimize these risks.

III.   OBJECTIONS TO FREE TRADE

In the last decade or so, public perturbations leading up to and surrounding meetings of the World Trade Organization and other international financial institutions, in particular the World Bank and the IMF, in Seattle, Washington, Quebec City and Genoa, supported

by a burgeoning anti-globalization literature,[13] have raised fundamental objections to free trade and economic liberalization. These
objections take various forms:

(a)   Globalization is leading to a global mono-culture.
(b)   Trade liberalization exacerbates inequalities of wealth between
      and within countries and threatens the welfare state.
(c)   Trade liberalization trumps environmental, health and safety,
      labour standards, and human rights concerns.
(d)   Trade liberalization undermines economic self-sufficiency in
      food production and other staples, creating dangerous depend-
      encies on foreigners.
(e)   The WTO is an undemocratic and unaccountable form of
      global government that improperly constrains domestic politi-
      cal sovereignty and democratic politics.

There are convincing refutations of most of these objections.[14]
In particular, it needs to be emphasized that trade liberalization
is likely to increase the total economic pie and average per capita
incomes by increasing economic productivity but says nothing
about what policies nation states should adopt to increase the productivity of citizens threatened by trade liberalization or to reduce
income inequality more generally. Arguably, the capacity of states to
underwrite such policies, if their citizens are so minded, is enhanced
rather than diminished by the greater wealth generated by trade
liberalization. Nevertheless, popular and scholarly debates over the
virtues and vices of economic globalization ensure that international

---

[13]   See e.g., Naomi Klein, *No Logo: Taking Aim at the Brand Bullies*
(Toronto: Vintage Canada, 2000) and *The Shock Doctrine: The Rise of
Disaster Capitalism* (Toronto: Vintage Canada, 2008); see also John Gray,
False Dawn: The Delusions of Global Capitalism (London: Granta Books,
2002); Joseph E. Stiglitz, *Making Globalization Work* (New York: W.W.
Norton & Co., 2006); Dani Rodrik, *The Globalization Paradox* (New York:
W.W. Norton, 2011).
[14]   See Jagdish N. Bhagwati, *In Defense of Globalization* (Oxford:
Oxford University Press, 2004); Philippe Legrain, *Open World: The
Truth About Globalization* (London: Abacus, 2002); Martin Wolf, *Why
Globalization Works* (New Haven: Yale University Press, 2004); Michael
Trebilcock, "Critiquing the Critics of Economic Globalization," (2005) 1 *J.
of International Law and International Relations* 213.

trade policy has forever forsaken the quiet and obscure corners of trade diplomacy that it once occupied, and become a matter of "high politics".

IV. INSTITUTIONAL HISTORY OF INTERNATIONAL TRADE POLICY

While international trade policy is commonly viewed as a post-World War II phenomenon, it has in fact a much longer genesis. During the latter half of the nineteenth century, nations such as France, Germany, and Britain negotiated bilateral trade treaties amongst themselves and with other European nations. In particular, Britain's resolute commitment to the principle of free trade was reflected in its unilateral removal or reduction of hundreds of tariffs on imported goods, beginning in the mid-nineteenth century with the repeal of the Corn Laws and lasting until the early years of the twentieth century. However, a severe recession in Europe in the 1870s resulted in many countries retreating from liberalized trade. The onset of World War I and the attendant disruption in trade relations, followed by the collapse of the world economy in the late 1920s, prompted many countries to adopt policies of extreme protectionism. The most dramatic example of such policies was the enactment of the Smoot-Hawley Tariff by the United States Congress in 1930, which raised average duties to 60 per cent on imported goods and provoked retaliatory measures by most of the U.S.'s trading partners. As a result of these "beggar-thy-neighbour" policies, international trade ground to a virtual standstill. Although the U.S. Congress signaled a shift in policy by passing the Reciprocal Trade Agreements Act in 1934, which gave the President authority to negotiate bilateral trade agreements, the outbreak of World War II shattered any hope of renewed international trade. As World War II wound down, post-war planners set their minds to the task of reconstructing the world economy after the war. As part of the Bretton Woods Agreement in 1944, they proposed the formation of the International Trade Organization (ITO) to oversee a new multilateral system of liberalized international trade (along with the IMF to stabilize international exchange rates and the World Bank to provide development assistance). However, the ITO never came into existence due to strong opposition to it from the U.S. Congress, which feared that the

ITO would entrench excessively on domestic sovereignty. Instead, a provisional agreement negotiated in 1947 amongst 23 major trading countries as a prelude to the ITO, the General Agreement on Tariffs and Trade (GATT), became by default the permanent institutional basis for today's world trade regime, now comprising more than 150 nations.[15]

Under the GATT, eight "rounds" of negotiations have now been completed. The first six of these rounds, up to and including the Kennedy Round which concluded in 1967, focused mainly on reciprocal reductions in tariffs on manufactured goods.[16] More recent rounds, including the Tokyo Rounds ending in 1979 and the Uruguay Round ending in 1993, have increasingly focused on non-tariff barriers to trade, such as government procurement policies, subsidy policies, customs valuations policies, health and safety and technical standards. From an institutional perspective, the Uruguay Round was particularly important in that it resulted in the creation of the World Trade Organization (WTO), the overarching governing body that had been missing from the world trade regime since the failure to create the ITO.

Recent developments in the GATT/WTO system have seen increasing strains being placed upon the world trade regime by a multitude of factors, including the dramatic increase in the number of members (now 153) in very different states of development. In addition, the inclusion of several new issues in trade negotiations that had previously been considered outside the ambit of the GATT, such as foreign investment, intellectual property, and trade in services, has entailed a greater focus on domestic policy divergences as potential distortions of international trade, and thus raised concerns about the degree to which GATT/WTO commitments on these issues may constrain domestic sovereignty. Contentious issues such as trade in agricultural products, which had previously largely escaped GATT discipline, are now also being addressed. As well, developing countries have shown an increased willingness to form coalitions in order to advance their collective interests during negotiations, as exemplified by the formation of the "Group of 21" voting block of

---

[15]   See Irwin, Mavroidis, and Sykes, *supra* note 9.
[16]   The success of these rounds is reflected in the fact that average world tariffs on manufactured goods have dropped from more than 40 per cent in 1947 to about 5 per cent today.

developing countries at the 2003 Cancun Ministerial meetings of the current Doha Round (launched in 2001).

V. GOVERNANCE AND DISPUTE SETTLEMENT IN THE WTO

The governance structure of the WTO system comprises the Ministerial Conference that meets every two years, a General Council comprised of delegates of all member countries and its various committees, the Secretariat headed by the Director-General who is appointed by consensus of the member states, and the quasi-judicial dispute settlement body.

The Agreement Establishing the World Trade Organization ("WTO Agreement") sets out various provisions for adjusting GATT commitments over time.[17] Article X:1 of the WTO Agreement requires that any proposal to amend a WTO agreement must be tabled for a minimum of 90 days before the agreement can be amended. Amendments to WTO agreements are voted on by the Ministerial Conference of the WTO. Article X:2 sets out specific provisions of WTO Agreements that can only be amended by unanimous agreement of all members. All other provisions can be amended by a two-thirds majority of the Ministerial Conference; however, such amendments are only binding on the members who have voted in favour of the amendment (Article X:3). This feature of the WTO Agreement is subject to Article X:5, which stipulates that the Ministerial Conference may decide by a three-fourths majority that an amendment is of such a nature that any member which has not accepted it within a period specified by the Ministerial Conference in each case shall be free to withdraw from the WTO or

---

[17]   For recent reviews of institutional challenges facing the WTO, see Report of the Consultative Board to the Director-General of the WTO (2004), *The Future of the WTO: Addressing Institutional Challenges in the New Millennium*; Debra P. Steger, "The Future of the WTO: The Case for Institutional Reform," (2009) 12 *J. of International Economic Law* 803; more generally, Debra P. Steger (ed.), *Redesigning the World Trade Organization for the Twenty-first Century* (Wilfrid Laurier University Press, Ontario, Canada, 2010); Tomer Broude, *International Governance in the WTO: Judicial Boundaries and Political Capitulation* (London: Cameron May, 2004).

to remain a member with the consent of the Ministerial Conference. Finally, Article IX:2 grants exclusive authority to the Ministerial Conference and the General Council to adopt authoritative, binding interpretations of the various WTO Agreements, provided that the proposed interpretation receives the support of three-fourths of the members. Finally, Article IX:3 of the WTO Agreement provides that in exceptional circumstances, the Ministerial Conference may decide to waive a WTO obligation of a member, provided that any such decision shall be taken by three-fourths of the members. Despite these formal voting rules, the convention has developed of most decisions being taken by "consensus" (meaning the absence of explicit objections).

With respect to specific disputes between members (which it must be emphasized are governments, not private parties), Article XXII of the GATT imposes an obligation on members to accord sympathetic consideration to complaints of other parties and adequate opportunity for consultation with such parties. If the members cannot resolve a dispute through mutual negotiations, perhaps assisted by mediation of a third party, including the Director-General of the GATT or his or her staff, the dispute must then be addressed within the framework of Article XXIII, now substantially elaborated on in the Uruguay Round Understanding on Rules and Procedures Governing the Settlement of Disputes. Under this Article, if a member considers that any benefit accruing to it directly or indirectly under the GATT is being "nullified or impaired" by a policy or practice of another member, the complaining member can refer its complaint to the members as a group (the General Council of the WTO acting as the dispute-settlement body), which will appoint a panel to investigate the complaint and make recommendations to the Council for resolution of the dispute. Panels typically comprise three individuals acting in their personal capacities, drawn from countries other than the disputing parties, who meet privately with the disputing parties to ascertain the facts and the precise nature of the allegation, and if possible to resolve the dispute informally. If this is not possible, the Panel will make recommendations to the Council as to the resolution of the matter. The Council makes decisions on Panel recommendations on a negative consensus basis, requiring consensus in favour of rejection of the Panel's recommendations (which would require the support of the prevailing member before the Panel, which means in practice that adoption of Panel decisions is automatic). Under the Dispute Settlement Understanding, Panel decisions may now be appealed on matters of law to a standing Appellate Body of seven members (sitting in panels of 3), whose decisions are subject to a similar negative consensus adoption rule in the WTO Council. If the Council adopts the recommendations of the Panel or the Appellate Body, then a member is required to modify or withdraw its policy or practice to bring itself into conformity with the Council's decision. If it fails to do so, the Council may authorize retaliatory action by the aggrieved member in the form of suspension of trade concessions or other obligations of equivalent value, the level of which is subject to arbitration in the event of disputes over the equivalence of proposed retaliatory measures. The dispute settlement regime under the GATT has evolved significantly since the genesis of the GATT in 1947, from relatively informal diplomatic forms of conciliation to much more formal and binding forms of quasi-judicial adjudication. This has led to vigorous contemporary debates over whether the quasi-judicial arms of the GATT (now the WTO) have become too powerful relative to the political organs of the WTO and whether various forms of institutional rebalancing are warranted.[18]

VI. PREFERENTIAL TRADE AGREEMENTS

Running parallel with the evolution of the multilateral trading system under the GATT in the post-war period has been another institutional development of considerable significance – the rise of preferential trading blocks. Since 1947, more than four hundred such arrangements have been notified to the GATT/WTO, including many in the past decade. The most important of these arrangements is the European Union, which began in 1957 under the Treaty of Rome with six initial members and now expanded to twenty-seven members (with other countries negotiating accession). Another such arrangement of considerable significance is the North American Free Trade Agreement (NAFTA) between the U.S., Canada and Mexico, which was entered into in 1992. Other regional trading blocks

---

[18] See Joost Pauwelyn, "The Transformation of World Trade," (2005) 104:1 *Michigan Law Review* 1; Steger, *supra* note 17.

have emerged in Latin America (MERCOSUR), the Caribbean (CARICOM), Asia (ASEAN) and Eastern and Southern Africa (COMESA). Such arrangements are permitted under Article XXIV of the GATT provided that they meet two conditions: (a) trade restrictions are eliminated with respect to substantially all trade between the member countries; and (b) customs duties shall not be higher thereafter than the duties prevailing on average throughout the constituent territories prior to the formation of the regional trading agreement. Article XXIV contemplates two different kinds of regional trading agreements: a free trade agreement, which leaves the contracting parties free to adopt their own trade and tariff policies with respect to the rest of the world, and a customs union, which involves not only liberalization of trade between the member countries but also requires that these countries adopt a common external tariff with regard to other countries. In these terms, the E.U. is a customs union while NAFTA is a free trade area.

In considering institutional arrangements to promote regional economic integration, it is useful to think of an integration continuum. First, there are free trade areas (like NAFTA), where two or more countries agree to remove border restrictions on goods amongst themselves, but each reserves the right to maintain whatever external trade policy it wishes with respect to non-member countries. A particular problem raised by this kind of arrangement is importation of goods through low tariff member countries and trans-shipment to higher tariff member countries, which can only be resolved with complex rules of origin that typically specify the extent of the product transformation or value-added required to have been undertaken in a country in order for a product to qualify as having originated in that country. Second, there are customs unions where, in addition to removing border restrictions on trade and goods among member countries, member countries also agree to harmonize their external trade policies vis-à-vis non-member countries. Third, there are common markets or economic unions, like the European Union, where, in addition to removing border restrictions on trade in goods among member countries and harmonizing external trade policy, free movement of services, capital and people, as well as perhaps a common monetary policy and currency, might be contemplated. Fourth, there are federalist structures, like the U.S., Canada, Australia, and Germany, where economic units form a single state, with the central government being vested with dominant jurisdiction over economic functions, but with some agreed division of economic powers between the central and sub-national levels of government, with constitutional or other arrangements designed to guarantee internal free movement of goods, services, capital, and people, and minimization of internal barriers to trade. Finally, there are unitary states where, over a given geographic region, one government, to all intents and purposes – with some exceptions for local governments – possesses exclusive jurisdiction over all significant economic functions, so that problems of inter-governmental coordination of economic policies within the geographic area are eliminated.[19]

While some analysts believe that preferential trading blocks and the multilateral system can be viewed as complementary and mutually reinforcing, other analysts consider them as inherently discriminatory and a major threat to the future stability and integrity of the multilateral system.[20]

VII. OVERVIEW OF THE SUBSTANTIVE PROVISIONS OF THE GATT/WTO

A. Tariffs

Under Article XXVIII bis of the GATT, members commit themselves to entering into periodic negotiations on a reciprocal and mutually advantageous basis, directed to the substantial reduction in the general level of tariffs. Once tariff concessions are agreed to in a particular set of negotiations, these become "tariff bindings", which are set out in particular members' tariff schedules that constitute an Annex to the GATT. By virtue of Article II of the GATT, all members must adhere to these tariff bindings by not imposing customs duties in excess of those set forth in each country's schedule. Article XXVIII of the GATT permits members to renegotiate their GATT tariff commitments periodically. Every three years,

---

19   See Michael J. Trebilcock and Robert Howse, *The Regulation of International Trade, 3rd edition* (Routledge, 2005) at 29–30.
20   See e.g., Jagdish Bhagwati, *Termites in the Trading System* (New York: Oxford University Press, 2008); Razeen Sally, *New Frontiers in Free Trade: Globalization's Future and Asia's Rising Role* (Washington, D.C.: Cato Institute, 2008), Chapter 5.

members may enter into negotiations with other concerned members to modify or withdraw tariff concessions previously made (Article XXVIII:1). Such negotiations must include provisions for compensating concessions to affected parties and must seek to maintain a general level of reciprocal and mutually advantageous concessions not less favourable to trade than that existing prior to such negotiations (Article XXVIII:2).

In terms of the domestic administration of tariffs (or customs duties), Article VII of the GATT requires that the value for customs purposes of imported merchandise should be based on its "actual value", a definition that has been elaborated on subsequently in a special Customs Valuation Code. Similarly, most members have agreed to harmonize their systems of customs classifications to reduce room for ambiguity or debate as to the proper tariff classification of a particular good. Finally, Article VIII of the GATT restricts the imposition of fees or charges related to the administrative processing of inbound goods to the approximate cost of services rendered.

B. Quantitative Restrictions

Article XI prohibits the use of quotas or import or export restrictions on the importation or exportation of goods into or out of any member state, reflecting the theory that if barriers to trade were expressed solely in the form of tariffs, the relative transparency of tariffs relative to quotas and other forms of quantitative restrictions would make possible their reduction over time through periodic negotiating rounds. However, there are a number of important exceptions to Article XI. First, Articles XII and XVIII permit members to impose quotas if they are experiencing balance of payment problems, and in the case of Article XVIII, if a developing country wishes to protect an infant industry. Second, since the 1980s there have been a number of bilateral "Voluntary" Export Restraint Agreements (VEAs) negotiated in clear violation of Article XI and usually under threat of unilateral action by the importing country. However, the Agreement on Safeguards negotiated during the Uruguay Round now largely prohibits the use of VEAs. A prime example of such a voluntary export agreement is the Multi-fibre Arrangement (MFA) governing trade in clothing and textiles. The Uruguay Round Agreement on Textiles and Clothing provides for the gradual removal of the quantitative restrictions provided for under the MFA.

C.   Non-discrimination

The principle of non-discrimination – often viewed as the corner-stone of the GATT – is referred to in the Preamble to the Agreement and is amplified in two key provisions: Article I, adopting the Most Favoured Nation (MFN) Principle; and Article III, adopting the National Treatment Principle. Under Article I of the GATT (MFN), with respect to customs duties or charges of any kind imposed by any country on any other member country, any advantage, favour, privilege, or immunity granted by such country to any product originating in any other country should be accorded immediately and unconditionally to a like-product originating in the territories of all other members. Thus, notwithstanding that tariff concessions may be principally negotiated between country A and country B, which may be the principal suppliers and purchasers of the products in question respectively, if either country A or country B makes a binding tariff concession to the other, it must extend exactly the same concession to all other members of the GATT/WTO, without being able to demand quid pro quos as a condition of the extension of this concession, at least if these were not part of the initial nego-tiations. The MFN Principle is designed to constrain discrimination by members amongst different foreign exporters, that is, playing favourites among foreigners.

The National Treatment Principle set out in Article III of the GAT addresses another form of discrimination, namely where a member adopts internal or domestic fiscal or regulatory policies designed to favour its domestic producers vis-à-vis foreign producers of like products, even though the latter may all be treated in a uniform way. The National Treatment Principle requires that once border duties have been paid by foreign exporters, as provided for in a country's tariff schedules, no additional burdens may be imposed through internal taxes or regulations, and so on, on foreign exporters where domestic producers of the like product do not bear the same burden.

With respect to both the Most Favoured Nation Principle and the National Treatment Principle, the issue of what constitutes "like products" has been the subject of a number of high profile GATT/WTO trade disputes.

D. State Trading Enterprises

Under Article XVII of the GATT, each member undertakes that its state trading enterprises (state-owned enterprises or private enterprises operating under state-conferred monopolies or privileges) shall, with respect to purchases or sales involving either imports or exports, act in a non-discriminatory manner and make such purchases or sales solely in accordance with commercial considerations. This provision does not apply to imports of products for immediate or ultimate consumption in governmental use and not otherwise for resale.

E. Subsidies

Government subsidies that affect international trade by artificially reducing the price of products have proven an intractable problem for the multilateral trading system. It is helpful to keep in mind a basic taxonomy of subsidy scenarios. The first scenario is where country A subsidizes its exports into country B's market. This is the scenario which has classically attracted the potential for countervailing duties under Article VI of the GATT and complementary domestic trade remedy laws. The second scenario is where country A subsidizes its exports to country C, and in so doing displaces country B's exports from country C's market. In this scenario the subsidized goods are not moving from country A to country B and thus cannot be countervailed by country B, so that country B is remitted to a complaint under the Uruguay Round Subsidies and Countervailing Measures Agreement (SCM Agreement) for resolution under the multilateral dispute resolution process. The third subsidy scenario is the case where country A is subsidizing its domestic producers to service principally country A's own domestic market, and in so doing displaces country B's exports to country A's market. Again, as in scenario two, the subsidized goods are not moving from country A to country B so as to attract possible countervailing duties in country B, so that country B is again remitted to the multilateral dispute resolution process under the SCM Agreement. This Agreement sets out detailed rules governing prohibited and actionable subsidies.

F. Government Procurement

The GATT initially exempted government procurement policies
from the National Treatment Principle under paragraph 8(a) of
Article III. However, under the Tokyo Round Code on Government
Procurement and the Uruguay Round Government Procurement
Agreement, the National Treatment principle applies to government procurement practices albeit with many exceptions and qualifications for state-owned enterprises and sub-national levels of
government, as well as financial thresholds for contracts to which
these principles apply. Moreover, the Government Procurement
Agreement is a plurilateral not multilateral agreement to which all
members of the WTO are committed, and has only 28 signatories.

G. Trade Remedies

Article VI of the GATT recognizes the right of members to take
unilateral action under domestic trade remedy laws where domestic
industries are being materially injured because of unfair foreign
trading practices, specifically either subsidization (discussed above)
or dumping. Dumping occurs in its most typical form where foreign
producers are selling goods into another country's market at prices
below those which they would normally charge in their home
market. Where this pricing practice is causing material injury (or a
threat thereof) to domestic producers of like products, antidumping
duties in the amount of the difference between the export market
price and the home market price may be imposed on the imported
goods. Article VI is amplified by an antidumping code initially negotiated during the Kennedy Round and revised in the course of the
Tokyo and Uruguay Rounds.

Where foreign government subsidization of exports is causing
material injury to a domestic industry producing like products in
the importing country, domestic trade remedy laws may permit
the unilateral imposition of countervailing duties on the subsidized
imports so as to off-set or neutralize these foreign subsidies. Again,
the rules governing countervailing duty actions are now subject to
a special code on subsidies initially negotiated during the Tokyo
Round and extensively revised during the Uruguay Round (the
SCM Agreement).

Unilateral trade measures may also be invoked as "safeguards".

Under Article XIX (commonly referred to as the safeguards or escape clause) if, as a result of unforeseen developments and of the effect of obligations incurred by a member under the GATT (including tariff concessions), any product that is being imported into the territory of that member in such increased quantities or under such conditions as to cause or threaten serious injury to domestic producers of like or directly competitive products in that territory, a member is entitled to suspend or modify obligations or concessions on a temporary basis in order to alleviate the injury. Unlike dumping and subsidization, the use of unilateral measures in this context is not seen as a response to "unfair" trade but to unexpected changes in circumstances. The rules governing safeguard actions have now been substantially refined and elaborated in the Uruguay Round Agreement on Safeguards.

H. Developing Countries

"Special and differential status" is accorded to developing countries under the GATT/WTO, both with respect to actions which they are permitted to take relating to imports and with respect to actions that developed countries are expected to take towards them with respect to their exports. Under Article XVIII, developing countries are given broader latitude to impose restrictions on imports, typically through quantitative restrictions such as quotas and licenses, for balance of payment reasons or in order to foster infant industries. Under Part IV of the GATT, added in 1966, Article XXXVI:A provides that developed countries do not expect reciprocity for commitments made by them in trade negotiations to reduce or remove tariffs and other barriers to the trade of less developed members. Article XXXVII, in turn, provides that developed countries commit themselves to according high priority to the non-reciprocal reduction and elimination of barriers to trade in products currently or potentially of export interest to less developed members. These latter provisions led to the introduction of the Generalized System of Preferences (GSP) in the early 1970s and the unilateral adoption of special preferences by many developed countries with respect to some exports of LDCs, initially under a waiver granted by GATT members and then subsequently a permanent Enabling Clause adopted in 1979 permitting exceptions to the MFN principle.

I. Exceptions to GATT Obligations

Under Article XXI of the GATT, various national security exceptions are provided for that permit a member to take any action
which it considers necessary for the protection of its essential security interests or which reflects the exigencies of war or other emergency in international relations.

International trade commitments entered into by federal states,
such as the U.S., Canada, Australia and Germany, pose a problem
in international trade law to the extent that commitments made
by national levels of government do not constitutionally bind sub-
national levels of government, who are not direct signatories of the
GATT and hence are not bound by GATT/WTO commitments
entered into by their national governments. Unitary states see this as
resulting in an unfair form of asymmetry in reciprocal commitments.
Article XXIV(12) of the GATT provides that each member shall
take such reasonable measures as may be available to it to ensure
observance of the provisions of this Agreement by regional and local
governments within its territories and has been interpreted strictly
by GATT panels, thus limiting the extent to which national governments can avoid the consequences of non-compliance with GATT
obligations by sub-national levels of government.

However, by far the most important set of exceptions to GATT
obligations in practice are contained in Article XX of the GATT,
which provides for a number of exceptions from GATT obligations
with respect to the adoption or enforcement by members of measures, for example, necessary to protect public morals; necessary to
protect human or animal health or life; necessary to secure compliance with laws or regulations which are not inconsistent with the
GATT; imposed for the protection of national treasures; or relating
to the conservation of exhaustible natural resources, provided that
none of these measures are applied so as to constitute an arbitrary
or unjustifiable form of discrimination between countries where the
same conditions prevail or a disguised restriction on international
trade. The exceptions provided for in Article XX and the conditions
limiting these exceptions set out in the Preamble or Chapeau of
Article XX have been the subject of a number of high-profile GATT/
WTO trade disputes.

J. Specialized Uruguay Round Agreements

Pursuant to the Uruguay Round negotiations that culminated in 1993, specialized agreements were entered into on agricultural trade liberalization (the Agreement on Agriculture); international trade in textiles and clothing (the Agreement on Textiles and Clothing); trade-related intellectual property rights (the TRIPS Agreement); trade-related investment measures (the TRIMS Agreement); international trade in services (the General Agreement on Trade in Services-GATS); health measures (the Sanitary and Phyto-sanitary Measures (SPS) Agreement), and technical barriers to trade (the Technical Barriers to Trade (TBT) Agreement). These agreements will be described in subsequent chapters.

VIII. THE DOHA ROUND

The Doha Round of multilateral negotiations, launched in November 2001, initially embraced a very ambitious negotiating agenda, including "new" issues such as trade and investment and trade and competition policy, but the agenda has become more modest over time (with investment and competition policy abandoned). Negotiations are currently stalled (perhaps fatally) over key issues regarding non-agricultural market access, agricultural trade liberalization, trade in services, and rules regarding antidumping, subsidies, countervailing duties, and regional trade agreements (but most acutely agricultural trade liberalization).[21]

---

[21]   See Paul Blustein, *Misadventures of the Most Favored Nations: Clashing Egos, Inflated Ambitions, and the Great Shambles of the World Trading System* (New York: PublicAffairs, 2009).

2. Dispute settlement under the GATT/WTO

I. HISTORY

In initial negotiations after World War II for the creation of a multilateral trading system, negotiating countries failed to adopt the Havana Charter, which would have led to the creation of the International Trade Organization (ITO). The GATT, as a provisional agreement, by default became a permanent framework for the multilateral trading system. It established an anemic institutional structure that member countries, by consensus, elaborated over time. Initial disputes were referred to the Chairman of the Contracting Parties for rulings on the legality of disputed measures – a process for which there was no provision in the GATT – and then evolved into the creation of five member Working Parties, comprising representatives of the two parties in dispute (member countries) and representatives of three other countries. These Working Parties were conceived as largely serving a diplomatic or conciliatory function where attempts were made to work out compromises acceptable to both disputing parties. In turn, by the mid-1950s Working Parties had evolved into something similar to the current Panels, typically comprising five individuals in their personal capacities and excluding representatives of the countries in dispute. These Panels would hear confidential written and oral submissions from the parties and make recommendations to the General Council of the GATT, which, by convention, required a positive consensus (including the acquiescence of the losing party) for their adoption. In the event of adoption, the contracting parties would recommend remedial measures to the party found in violation of its GATT obligations and in the event of failure to adopt such measures could authorize the aggrieved party to impose retaliatory sanctions against the party in violation, typically in the form of tariffs or quotas on imports from the latter. This process found its legal authority, such as it was, in Article

XXII of the GATT, prescribing initial consultations with a view to mutually acceptable resolutions of disputes, and in Article XXIII of the GATT, authorizing the Contracting Parties to investigate complaints of "nullification or impairment" of benefits expected under the Agreement in the event of failure of consultations, to recommend resolutions of disputes, and to authorize retaliatory sanctions in the event of failure to adopt such measures (although neither Article XXII nor Article XXIII in fact mention Panels).

Despite this rather fragile and ad hoc basis for resolving complaints, almost 300 complaints were filed with the GATT (many of them referred to Panels) between 1948 and 1989. A study of these cases by Robert Hudek et al.[1] found that it took about two years to resolve a dispute from the time a complaint was filed to the implementation of remedial measures. They also find a perhaps surprisingly high compliance rate for successful complaints of 88 per cent, with some decline in the compliance record in the 1980s to 81 per cent, which decade witnessed an explosion of complaints. For the entire 42-year period studied, 73 per cent of all complaints were filed by the U.S., the E.U. and its members, Canada, and Australia. The U.S., the E.U. and its member countries, Canada and Japan accounted for 83 per cent of all appearances as defendants. Of all complaints, 92 per cent involved either the U.S. or the E.U. (or its members) as a party. For the entire period, 52 per cent of all complaints related to non-tariff barriers (NTBs), 21 per cent to tariffs, 16 per cent to subsidies, and 10 per cent to antidumping/countervailing duty (AD/CVD) measures. Over time, NTBs and AD/CVDs increased as a percentage of complaints while tariffs sharply declined; in the 1950s, only 23 per cent of all complaints involved agricultural trade, while for the period 1960 to 1984, one half of the complaints involved agricultural trade measures, many relating to the E.U.'s Common Agricultural Policy.

However, despite, in many ways, the relative effectiveness of this dispute settlement regime, a number of countries (especially the U.S.) became dissatisfied with the functioning of the dispute-settlement system. In particular, these countries were critical of the ability of parties to engage in strategic foot-dragging in the appointment of

---

[1]   Robert E. Hudek, Daniel L. M. Kennedy and Mark Sgarbossa, "A Statistical Profile of GATT Dispute Settlement Cases, 1948 to 1989", (1993) 2 *Minnesota Journal of Global Trade* 1.

panels, settlement of their terms of reference, and adoption of their findings, given the ability of a party seeking to resist formal dispute settlement in effect to exercise veto rights at any of these critical decision junctures through the operation of the positive consensus rule. Hence, during the Uruguay Round (1986 to 1993), a concerted effort was made to strengthen the dispute-settlement system, resulting in the Dispute Settlement Understanding (DSU) that came into force in 1995 with the creation of the World Trade Organization. The principal modifications to the dispute-settlement system made by the DSU fall into three broad categories: a) strict deadlines on various stages in the consultation and dispute-settlement process; b) replacement of the positive consensus rule with a negative consensus rule, meaning that Panel and Appellate Body decisions were deemed to be adopted by the General Council of the WTO in the absence of a consensus favouring rejection, which would entail the prevailing party acquiescing in the rejection of a decision in its favour. This has meant that Panel (and Appellate Body) decisions are now adopted automatically by the WTO General Council; c) the creation of a standing Appellate Body of seven members, which sits in panels of three and has jurisdiction to hear appeals on matters of law from ad hoc Panel decisions.

II. THE CONTEMPORARY COMPLAINTS PROCESS[2]

The contemporary complaints process typically follows the following sequence:

1. The complaining party must initially engage in consultations with the party whose measures are in dispute. If the parties fail to settle a dispute (with the assistance of mediation if requested) within 60 days of the request for consultations, then the complaining member can request the establishment of a Panel.

---

[2] See generally, Henrik Horn and Petros Mavroidis, "International Trade: Dispute Settlement," in Andrew T. Guzman and Alan O. Sykes (eds.), *Research Handbook in International Economic Law* (Cheltenham, UK: Edward Elgar, 2007).

2. A Panel must be established at the meeting of the Dispute Settlement Body (the General Council of the WTO) following the meeting at which the request for a Panel first appears on the Dispute Settlement Body agenda.

3. Standard terms of reference are typically adopted for Panels unless the disputing parties agree otherwise within 20 days from the establishment of a Panel.

4. Panel members are typically drawn from a roster maintained by the Dispute Settlement Body with the consensus of member countries. If disputing parties cannot agree on panelists within 20 days of the establishment of a Panel, the Director-General of the WTO shall appoint panelists who may not be citizens of countries involved in the dispute. Other countries with a substantial interest in the matter can participate as Third Parties in Panel proceedings.

5. Under Article 11 of the DSU, a Panel's functions are to make an objective assessment of the facts and the applicability of relevant agreements to the facts and to present their findings and recommendations to the Dispute Settlement Body.

6. In Panel proceedings, the complaining party files its written submissions first, followed by written submissions from the responding party. Typically there is then one oral meeting with the Panel, then written rebuttal submissions are submitted, followed by a second oral meeting with the Panel. The Panel will then present to the parties a summary of their arguments and the factual description of the issues in contention for their comments. This is then typically followed by the presentation to the parties of an interim report by the Panel for the parties' comments. Following receipt of their comments, the Panel typically then prepares a final report. Proceedings before Panels are not normally to take longer than six months from the striking of a Panel to the issuance of a final report to the parties.

7. Panel reports are to be adopted by the Dispute Settlement Body within 60 days of circulation of the report to members, unless there is a negative consensus favouring rejection of the report, or the Panel's decision is appealed to the Appellate Body.

8. The parties may appeal panel decisions to the Appellate Body on matters of law and the Appellate Body is required to report within 60 days from notification of an appeal. The Appellate

Body's report is to be adopted by the Dispute Settlement Body within 30 days of circulation to members, unless there is a negative consensus favouring rejection.

9. Members have a reasonable period to comply with Panel or Appellate Body rulings, once adopted by the Dispute Settlement Body, but this period is not normally to exceed 15 months and is to be determined by arbitration failing agreement of the parties.

10. Where there is disagreement as to whether measures taken to comply with rulings in fact constitute compliance, the matter can be remitted to the original Panel (and potentially the Appellate Body on appeal) under Article 21.5 of the DSU.

11. If non-compliance persists, the Dispute Settlement Body may authorize retaliatory trade sanctions which typically involve the withdrawal of equivalent trade concessions, the issue of equivalence being subject to arbitration under Article 22.4.

III.   UTILIZATION OF THE NEW DISPUTE-SETTLEMENT PROCESS

Kara Leitner and Simon Lester have for a number of years prepared an annual cumulative analysis of WTO dispute-settlement proceedings since the institution of the new dispute-settlement process in 1995. Their latest analysis[3] reports the following basic statistics on utilization of the new dispute settlement system.

As of 1 January 2008 there have been 369 WTO complaints filed under the DSU since 1995, involving a total of 273 matters. The leading complaining parties have been the U.S. (with 88 complaints), the E.U. (with 76 complaints), Canada (with 29 complaints) and Brazil (with 23 complaints). In terms of responding parties, the U.S. has been the principal respondent in 99 disputes and the E.U. the second most frequent respondent in 59 disputes. That is to say, the U.S. or the E.U. has been the complaining party in 44 per cent of total complaints and the responding party in 43 per cent of total complaints. However, increasingly other countries have become

---

[3]   Kara Leitner and Simon Lester, "WTO Dispute Settlement 1995 to 2007 – A Statistical Analysis," (2008) 11:1 *Journal of International Economic Law* 179.

significant participants in the dispute-settlement system, including developing countries. Between 1995 and 2007, 234 complaints were filed by high-income countries, 86 by upper-middle-income countries, 40 by lower-middle-income countries, and 25 by low-income countries. Numbers for respondents are roughly comparable. However, there are enduring concerns that many developing countries lack the capacity to participate effectively in the increasingly complex dispute-settlement system and even where they prevail may lack effective retaliatory sanctions against much larger countries.[4] In terms of issues that are most frequently disputed, general GATT provisions account for the overwhelming number of issues in dispute at 281, followed by subsidies and countervailing measures issues at 78, antidumping duties at 72, and agricultural trade issues at 59.

Since the institution of the new dispute-settlement system in 1995, 115 Panel reports and 70 Appellate Body reports have been issued. The percentage of Panel reports appealed to date to the Appellate Body is 68 per cent.

IV. CRITICAL ISSUES IN EVALUATING THE DISPUTE-SETTLEMENT SYSTEM IN WORLD TRADE LAW

In many respects, the GATT/WTO dispute-settlement system is the envy of many other international legal regimes that lack any or effective enforcement regimes. A critical threshold question is why the GATT/WTO dispute-settlement system has worked relatively well over the course of the history of the GATT/WTO, despite some highly idiosyncratic features of the system, at least compared to domestic judicial dispute-settlement processes, especially prior to the 1995 reforms when the positive consensus rule applied. Even under the new system, why do parties mostly comply with adverse rulings, despite the absence of a supra-national Leviathan that can forcibly compel compliance? A related question is whether the evolution of the GATT/WTO dispute-settlement system from a diplomatically-oriented conciliation process to a much more

---

[4] See Chad P. Bown, *Self-enforcing Trade: Developing Countries and WTO Dispute Settlement* (Washington, DC: Brookings Institution, 2009).

formal, adversarial, quasi-judicial process is in every respect desirable?[5]

Reform proposals tend to fall into two broad categories – those that seek to strengthen the existing dispute-settlement system, and those that seek to retrench it relative to the political decision-making organs of the WTO, each of which needs to be carefully analyzed and debated. Proponents of strengthening the dispute settlement system advance various reform proposals:

a) Greater transparency in dispute-settlement proceedings by making written submissions of the parties available to the public when filed and making oral proceedings before Panels and the Appellate Body (subject to confidentiality protections) open to the public;

b) Expanding the opportunities for participation by non-state inter-venors through the filing of *amicus curiae* briefs and perhaps participation in oral hearings before Panels and the Appellate Body;

c) Permitting private parties to initiate complaints under the WTO dispute settlement regime, which it must be emphasized has hith-erto been exclusively the preserve of state-to-state complaints;

d) Providing that GATT/WTO rules have "direct effect" in the domestic legal systems of member states (as in the E.U.), where private parties can assert those rules in domestic legal proceed-ings, presumably subject to some kind of appeal process to the WTO dispute-settlement system (akin to appeals to the European Court of Justice in the E.U.) so that the GATT/WTO becomes a kind of global constitution;

e) Strengthening remedies for non-compliance with dispute-settlement rulings by, for example:

i) providing for monetary compensation for past losses (including legal costs, at least in the case of developing countries) and perhaps future losses in the event of continu-ing non-compliance, as an alternative to retaliation, which may be of limited efficacy for small countries that prevail in disputes against much larger countries;[6]

---

[5] See Pauwelyn *supra* Chapter 1, note 18 at 1; Tomer Broude, *International Governance in the World Trade Organization: Judicial Boundaries and Political Capitulation* (London: Cameron May, 2004).

[6] For a critique, see Alan O. Sykes, "Optimal Sanctions in the WTO:

ii) disproportionate or non-equivalent retaliation as a form of punishment or punitive damages to deter violations, as opposed to equivalent retaliation that might be thought to facilitate some violations, which some commentators view as efficient breaches if the benefits of breach exceed the costs to other parties;[7]

iii) tradeable retaliation rights that small countries could trade to larger countries who may be able more effectively to exercise these rights;

iv) collective retaliation rights/obligations, where all member countries are obliged or entitled to adopt retaliatory sanctions against another member's violation, whether they are directly affected or not.

Proponents of retrenching the dispute-settlement system on the grounds that it has grown too powerful relative to the political decision-making organs of the WTO and reflects excessive judicial activism or law-making argue that Panel or Appellate Body decisions should not be adopted if some significant minority, for example, one-third, of member countries object to a decision.[8] Complementary proposals are sometimes advanced for facilitating or streamlining decision-making by the political organs of the WTO. For example, there have been proposals to move away from a consensus rule of decision-making to more formal majority or supra-majority voting, with voting rights perhaps weighted by trade volumes (somewhat akin to weighted voting rights in the E.U.), and perhaps the appointment or election of a representative Executive Committee of the WTO to make a broad range of decisions without requiring the direct participation or endorsement of all 153 members (a form of delegated decision-making).

The Case for Decoupling (and the Uneasy Case for the Status Quo)," Stanford Law School, Law and Economics Olin Working Paper, No. 379, 2009.

[7] For a critique, see Warren F. Schwartz and Alan O. Sykes, "The Economic Structure of Renegotiation and Dispute Resolution in the World Trade Organization," (2002) 31:1 *J. of Legal Studies* 179.

[8] See Claude E. Barfield, *Free Trade, Sovereignty, Democracy: The Future of the World Trade Organization* (AEI Press, 2001); for a critical review of these proposals, see Debra P. Steger, "Free Trade, Sovereignty, Democracy: The Future of the World Trade Organization," (2002) 5:2 *J. of International Economic Law* 565.

3. Tariffs and the Most Favoured Nation Principle

I. THE ECONOMIC (WELFARE) EFFECTS OF A TARIFF

In the case of a prohibitive tariff, where imports are completely priced out of an importing country's market, domestic producers are likely to price up to the tariff, consumers in these countries who remain in the market will pay more for the domestically produced goods than they otherwise would without the tariff, and some consumers will be priced out of the market (often referred to as a dead-weight social cost). Consumers in importing countries lose more than producers in these countries gain (by virtue of this dead-weight social cost), thus reducing domestic welfare. Adverse impacts on foreign exporters of these goods also make the tariff globally welfare-reducing. In the case of a non-prohibitive tariff, governments in the importing country collect some revenue from the tariff, but this is almost never sufficient to off-set the negative impact of the tariff on domestic consumers or to produce a net welfare improvement in the importing country. Further, foreign exporters are adversely affected through changing the terms of trade.

The welfare effects of a tariff need to be considered relative to other protectionist instruments – in particular, quantitative restrictions and subsidies. In the case of quantitative restrictions, depending on how import quotas are allocated, domestic recipients of these quotas may realize scarcity rents from the quotas, or if the quotas are allocated to foreign exporters the latter are likely to realize scarcity rents from the quotas. However, as in the case of a non-prohibitive tariff, these benefits are highly unlikely to offset the negative impacts on domestic consumers from higher prices, and may exacerbate them relative to a non-prohibitive tariff that permits more efficient foreign exporters to surmount the tariff. Quantitative restrictions are banned under Article XI of the GATT, with numerous exceptions which must be applied on a non-discriminatory basis under Article XIII. With respect to domestic production subsidies that render domestically produced products artificially competitive with lower-priced imports, consumers will not face distorted prices relative to the prevailing world price for the product, but the subsidies will attract excessive resources into the domestic industry. In the case of both tariffs and quantitative restrictions, these distort both consumption and production decisions in importing countries.

II. INTERNATIONAL TARIFF NEGOTIATIONS

The preamble to the GATT commits members to enter into reciprocal and mutually advantageous arrangements directed to the substantial reduction of tariffs and other barriers to trade and to the elimination of discriminatory treatment in international commerce. Article XXVIII bis further provides that "members recognize that customs duties often constitute serious obstacles to trade and that negotiations on a reciprocal and mutually advantageous basis, directed to the substantial reduction of the general level of tariffs are of great importance to the expansion of international trade." Pursuant to these provisions, eight rounds of multilateral negotiations have been concluded to date, with a ninth round – the Doha Round – currently in progress. Over the course of these rounds, tariffs on industrial goods have been reduced worldwide on average from over 40 per cent in 1947 to a little more than 3 per cent today. There are significant remaining tariffs on industrial goods from country to country on particular classes of goods, and extremely high tariffs on particular agricultural products that often run, in the case of many countries, to several hundred per cent. Negotiations over tariff reductions have adopted different negotiating principles over time. The first five negotiating rounds adopted product-by-product negotiations, which were extremely transaction-cost intensive. Later rounds adopted some combination of linear cuts and exceptions which were negotiated on a product-by-product basis, typically with further agreement that in the case of linear cuts countries with high tariffs should cut by deeper percentages than countries with already lower tariffs. The reduction of tariffs on industrial goods worldwide has been perhaps the most important achievement of the GATT over the course of its history.

Once tariff negotiations have been concluded, these become tariff bindings which are set out in particular members' tariff schedules that constitute an Annex to the GATT. By virtue of Article II of the GATT, all parties must adhere to these tariff bindings by not imposing custom duties in excess of those set forth in each country's tariff binding schedule. This is subject to an exception provided for in Article XXVIII, where at scheduled three-yearly intervals, any member that has made previous tariff concessions can reopen these concessions with other members who have a substantial interest in the concession, with a view to modifying or withdrawing the concession. The member reopening tariff concessions must offer other concessions so that a general level of reciprocal, mutually advantageous concessions not less favourable to trade than those existing between the parties prior to such reopening is maintained.

III. DOMESTIC ADMINISTRATION OF TARIFFS

Four issues are required to be addressed in the domestic administration of tariffs.

A. Valuation of Imported Goods

Most tariffs today are *ad valorem* tariffs, requiring the importer to pay a certain percentage of the good's value in duty. Thus, valuation of the imported goods is an important determinant of the ultimate import duty. Article VII of the GATT requires parties to the Agreement to base value for customs purposes of imported merchandise on the actual value of the imported merchandise and not on the value of merchandise of national origin or on arbitrary or fictitious values. During the Tokyo and Uruguay Rounds a Customs Valuation Agreement was negotiated that seeks to elaborate a detailed set of valuation rules, establishing as the primary standard of valuation "transaction value," which is the price paid or payable for the goods when sold for export to the country of importation, plus certain additions such as the cost of packaging and the value of various items provided to the buyer free of charge in connection with the sale of the goods. Alternative methods of valuation are provided where transaction value is inappropriate, such as sales between related parties.

B.   Classification

Because there is a wide variation in the level of tariffs from product to product, goods must be located in the correct product category in a country's tariffs schedule to receive appropriate tariff treatment. A detailed harmonized classification system has now evolved that attempts to reduce both ambiguity and opportunism in the classification of imported goods.

C.   Rules of Origin

Because tariff rates often vary depending on where the goods originate, rules of origin are often required in order to determine the country of origin. For example, Canada has five major tariff treatments, depending on where goods originate: the general tariff on non-members of the GATT/WTO; the MFN rate under the GATT; the NAFTA rate for imports from the other two NAFTA members; the GSP rate for imports from developing countries to whom preferences have been extended; and a small residual category for preferences, such as preferences to other British Commonwealth countries, prevailing at the inception of the GATT. In the contemporary global economy, where goods or components thereof are often produced in many different countries, rules of origin are often exceptionally complex and somewhat arbitrary. Little progress has been made towards harmonizing these rules both within countries in different trade policy contexts, and between or among countries.

D.   Customs Fees and Administration

Article VIII of the GATT restricts the imposition of fees or charges related to the administrative processing of inbound goods to the approximate cost of services rendered, which must not represent an indirect protection to domestic producers or a taxation of imports for fiscal purposes.

IV. THE MOST FAVOURED NATION PRINCIPLE

Once tariff commitments have been agreed to in tariff negotiations and become tariff bindings under Article II of the GATT, these must be extended to all members of the GATT/WTO system under the Most Favoured Nation Principle set out in Article I, which is why the MFN Principle is often viewed as the cornerstone of the multilateral trading system (in contrast to a system of bilateral deals). Article I provides:

> With respect to customs duties and charges of any kind imposed on or in connection with importation or exportation or imposed on the international transfer of payments for imports for exports, and with respect to the method of levying such duties and charges, and with respect to all rules and formalities in connection with importation and exportation, and with respect to all matters referred to in paragraphs 2 and 4 of Article III, any advantage, favour, privilege or immunity granted by any Contracting Party to any product originating in or destined for any other country shall be accorded immediately and unconditionally to the like product originating in or destined for the territories of all other Contracting Parties.

This principle is subject to a number of exceptions, the most important of which relate to preferential trading agreements, and GSP preferences for developing countries. However, before moving to a discussion of these important exceptions, I first explore the theoretical rationales for the MFN Principle, and then a number of important interpretive issues that have arisen in its application and have engaged the dispute settlement system under the GATT/WTO.

A.   Theoretical Rationales for the MFN Principle

A political justification for the MFN principle relates to the reduction of factionalism by constraining countries from engaging in playing favourites amongst foreigners for foreign policy or national security reasons, which were thought to have severely exacerbated international tensions leading up to World War II. However, in a contemporary setting, the principal rationales for the MFN Principle relate to the economic or welfare properties of the principle, and in this respect three such properties have been identified in the theoretical literature.[1]

1. Constraining bilateral opportunism in sequenced concessions favouring participating third parties

Here the scenario involves A and B trading tariff concessions, and B subsequently making more favourable concessions to C. Under the MFN Principle the more favourable concessions that B grants to C must also be extended to A. In the absence of the MFN Principle, A would have to contemplate the risk of B making more favourable concessions subsequently to C, and might then make less substantial concessions to B in the first round of negotiations, or withhold concessions altogether, preventing the conclusion of a mutually beneficial agreement. This kind of concern was very much evident in successive negotiations over the Canada–U.S. Free Trade Agreement in the late 1980s, which was then largely superseded by NAFTA between Canada, the U.S. and Mexico in the early 1990s. If Canada had declined to participate in the subsequent negotiations over NAFTA, it risked losing the benefits of preferential access to the U.S. markets negotiated under the Canada–US Free Trade Agreement if the U.S. and Mexico were to negotiate more favourable concessions with each other with respect to access to each other's markets, hence largely forcing Canada's hand in participating in the subsequent negotiations.

2. Constraining bilateral opportunism disadvantaging non-participating third parties

Here the concern is that when two parties (A and B) negotiate tariff or related concessions with one another, while liberalizing trade between themselves (trade creation), this may disadvantage non-participating third parties (e.g., C) with respect to access to either A or B's markets (trade diversion). Trade may be diverted away from C to either A or B who are parties to this arrangement. More extremely, A and B may negotiate a bilateral agreement between themselves which takes the form of a customs union, which enables

---

[1] See Warren F. Schwartz and Alan O. Sykes, "Towards a Positive Theory of the Most Favoured Nation Obligation and its Exceptions in the WTO/GATT System," (1996) 16 *International Review of Law and Economics* 27; and Kyle Bagwell and Robert W. Staiger, *supra* Chapter 1, note 6, at 5.

them to raise common duties vis-à-vis non-participating third parties and change the terms of trade vis-à-vis these parties in effect by exercising monopsony power against them. Article XXIV of the GATT, in dealing with free trade agreements and customs unions, attempts to constrain these effects by requiring that countries to such arrangements (a) substantially eliminate restrictions on all trade between or among themselves (the internal condition), and (b) not raise average duties subsequent to entering into such a bilateral arrangement vis-à-vis third parties relative to the average duties that prevailed during the negotiation of such an arrangement (the external condition).

3. The free rider problem

Where A and B negotiate tariffs or related concessions between themselves, under the MFN Principle C is not required to provide any quid pro quo for receipt of identical benefits and is in effect a free-rider on the concessions that A and B have made to each other. This weakens the negotiating position of A or B in subsequent negotiations with C and may reduce incentives for A or B to make initial concessions to each other. Because the MFN Principle does not contemplate complete reciprocity, this is part of the motivation that explains the proliferation of preferential trade agreements between much smaller numbers of parties in the post-war years (discussed in the next chapter).

While theoretical rationales for the MFN Principle present something of a mixed balance sheet, nevertheless it needs to be acknowledged that tariff negotiations, at least with respect to industrial goods, under the GATT have been its most signal achievement.

B. Interpretive Issues in the Application of the MFN Principle

1. Scope of Article I

Case law has made it clear that the MFN Principle applies not only to imports but exports, and applies not only to tariffs but to various rules and formalities applicable to imports and to internal taxes and regulatory measures that are covered by Article III (2) and (4) of the GATT (the National Treatment Principle).

2. Unconditionality

This has been a major matter of contention in a long line of trade disputes that have come before the Dispute Settlement Body of the

GATT/WTO. Various interpretations have been adopted of the requirement that all advantages, favours, privileges, and immunities extended by one Contracting Party to another should be immediately and unconditionally extended to all other members. One interpretation is that no conditions can be imposed that require other countries to provide quid pro quos. Another interpretation is that no conditions at all can be attached to the extension of MFN treatment. A yet further interpretation is that conditions are permitted but cannot discriminate by country of origin. A further possible interpretation is that conditions are permitted but that these must relate to the characteristics of the goods themselves (and not, for example, to differences in production and processing methods – PPMs).

In the *Belgium – Family Allowances* case (1952),[2] Belgian law imposed a charge on foreign goods purchased by public bodies when these goods originated in a country whose system of family allowances did not meet specific requirements that rendered their system comparable to that in place in Belgium. A number of countries had been granted an advantage – that is, an exemption – from the levy, but not others. A GATT panel held that conditioning the imposition of this internal tax on what kind of system of family allowances foreign countries had adopted violated Article I, in that this condition had nothing to do with the nature of the goods in question. In the *Indonesia – Auto* case (1998),[3] various exemptions from customs duties and internal taxes turned on various conditions and criteria not related to the nature of the imports themselves but rather, in effect, to the country of origin. The panel held that these conditions discriminated on the basis of country of origin and not product characteristics and hence violated Article I. In the *Canada – Auto* case (2000),[4] various duty remission rules on imported cars were conditioned on the manufacturers meeting various domestic content requirements in the production of other cars. Here the panel, after

---

[2] *Belgian Family Allowances (allocations familiales)*, adopted 7 November 1952, G/32 - BISD 1S/59 [*Belgium – Family Allowances* 1952].

[3] *Indonesia – Certain Measures Affecting the Automobile Industry*, WT/DS54/R, WT/DS55/R, WT/DS59/R, WT/DS64/R and Corr. 1, 2, 3 and 4, adopted 23 July 1998, DSR 1998; VI, 2201. [*Indonesia – Autos* 1998].

[4] *Canada – Certain Measures Affecting the Automotive Industry*, WT/DS139/R, WT/DS142/R, adopted 19 June 2000, as modified by the Appellate Body Report, WT/DS139/AB/R, WT/DS142/AB/R [*Canada – Automobiles* 2000].

analyzing the *Indonesia – Auto* case, concluded that the fact that conditions are attached to a particular advantage and are not related to the imported product itself does not necessarily imply that such conditions are discriminatory with respect to the origin of imported products. This seems to imply that only conditions that discriminate on the basis of origin (and not, e.g., differences in PPMs) violate Article I.

3. Like products
The MFN Principle only requires that any advantage, favour, privilege or immunity extended to one class of product from an exporting country be extended to exporters of like products from other foreign countries. The concept of "like products" has been enormously contentious both in the GATT/WTO case law and in scholarly commentary. Some cases, particularly in disputes over tariff classifications, have adopted quite narrow interpretations of like product, essentially requiring products to be (almost) identical in their physical characteristics. This view is reflected in the panel decisions in *Australia – Ammonium Sulphate* (1950),[5] *Germany – Sardines* (1952),[6] *EC – Animal Feed Protein* (1978),[7] and *Japan – SPF Dimension Lumber* (1989)[8] (which involved different species of soft-wood lumber used in home construction and which were held not to be "like" products). Other cases have taken a broader, more functional approach to the interpretation of like product, applying something closer to an antitrust law conception of whether given products fall into a relevant product market, which largely turns on their degree of functional substitutability from the perspective of consumers of those products despite significant physical differences (e.g., butter and margarine). Cases that appear to favour this

---

[5] Working Party Report, *The Australian Subsidy on Ammonium Sulphate*, GATT/CP.4/39, adopted 3 April 1950, BISD II/188 [*Australia – Ammonium Sulphate* 1950].

[6] *Treatment by Germany of Imports of Sardines*, adopted 31 October 1952, G/26 - BISD 1S/53 [*Germany – Sardines* 1952].

[7] *EEC – Measures on Animal Feed Proteins*, adopted 14 March 1978, L/4599 - BISD 25S/49 [*EEC – Animal Feed Proteins* 1978].

[8] *Canada/Japan – Tariff on Imports of Spruce, Pine, Fir (SPF) Dimension Lumber*, adopted 19 July 1989, L/6470 - BISD 36S/167 [*Japan – SPF Dimension Lumber* 1989].

view include *Spain – Unroasted Coffee* (1981),[9] – different species of coffee were treated as like products – and *Indonesia – Autos* (1998).[10] An argument favouring narrow interpretations of the like product requirement in Article I is that tariff negotiations, which depend on reciprocity, put a high premium on issues of manageability and reciprocity in tariff administration. Products should not be defined so broadly that a variety of third countries who have offered no quid pro quos are able to benefit from tariff concessions (the free rider problem). An argument for a broader functional conception of like products is that it can be more coherently and consistently applied, as in antitrust law, than simply comparing the physical character-istics of products. An important policy issue that flows from this difference in approaches to the interpretation of the like product requirement is whether countries are able to distinguish or discrimi-nate between imported products on the basis of differences in pro-duction and processing methods (e.g., with respect to differences in labour or environmental standards in the exporting country).

4. De facto discrimination
A number of cases have now recognized that Article I applies not only to de jure or explicit forms of discrimination between or amongst foreign imports but also to forms of de facto discrimination (*EC – Beef from Canada* (1981);[11] *Spain – Unroasted Coffee* (1981);[12] *EC – Bananas* (1999);[13] *Indonesia – Automobiles* (1998);[14] *Canada – Automobiles* (2000)[15]). Thus, a domestic measure that is facially neutral as amongst imports from different foreign countries may nevertheless have a disparate impact on imports of like products (however defined) from some foreign countries relative to others.

---

[9]   *Spain – Tariff Treatment of Unroasted Coffee*, adopted 11 June 1981, L/5135 – BISD 28S/102 [*Spain – Unroasted Coffee* 1981].
[10]   *Indonesia – Autos* 1998, *supra* note 3.
[11]   *European Economic Community – Imports of Beef from Canada*, adopted 10 March 1981, L/5099 - BISD 28S/92 [*EC – Beef from Canada* 1981].
[12]   *Spain – Unroasted Coffee* 1981, *supra* note 39.
[13]   *European Communities – Regime for the Importation, Sale and Distribution of Bananas – Recourse to Article 21.5 by the European Communities*, 12 April 1999, WT/DS27/RW/EEC [*EC – Bananas* 1999].
[14]   *Indonesia – Autos* 1998, *supra* note 3.
[15]   *Canada – Automobiles*, 2000, *supra* note 4.

This interpretation seems obviously necessary to prevent formalistic circumventions of the MFN requirement.

5. MFN obligations under Article XIII of the GATT
Under Article XIII of the GATT, "no prohibition or restriction (such as quotas) shall be applied by any Contracting Party on the importation of any product of the territory of any other Contracting Party or on the exportation of any product destined for the territory of any other Contracting Party, unless the importation of the like product of all third parties or the exportation of the like product to all third countries is similarly prohibited or restricted."

In *EC – Bananas III* (1999),[16] among several other MFN complaints, the complainants (the U.S. and various Latin American countries) claimed that the E.C. regime for the allocation of tariff rate quotas (TRQs) with respect to bananas violated Article XIII. The EC – Banana import regime established three categories of bananas imports: (1) traditional ACP bananas (from Lomé Convention ex-colonies in Africa, the Caribbean, and the Pacific); (2) third country bananas; and (3) non-traditional ACP bananas. Quotas were allocated to each of these categories, heavily favouring category (1). The E.C. had previously been granted a waiver from the MFN provisions of the GATT in Article I with respect to its Lomé Convention obligations to former colonies in the Caribbean, Latin America, and Africa. However, the Appellate Body held that the exemption from Article I did not also imply an exemption from Article XIII and held that the allocation of tariff rate quotas violated Article XIII.

V. CONCLUSIONS

While the MFN principle has often been called the "corner-stone" of the multilateral trading system, two major exceptions to the principle increasingly challenge its pre-eminence: first, the proliferation of Preferential Trade Agreements (PTAs), negotiated on a bilateral, regional, or cross-regional basis amongst sub-sets of members of the WTO, that by their nature treat members more favourably than non-members; and second, special and differential treatment

---

16   *European Communities – Bananas III,* 1999, *supra* note 13.

of developing countries, including the existence of unilateral, non-reciprocal preference to many such countries by developed countries. Both of these phenomena are sufficiently important to warrant treatment in separate chapters of this book.

4. Preferential trade agreements

I. INTRODUCTION

Preferential trade agreements (PTAs) are treaties between two or more countries granting preferential market access to each other's markets. PTAs may be bilateral, regional, or cross-regional. PTAs have proliferated rapidly in recent years. Since 1948, 474 PTAs have been notified to the GATT/WTO, amongst which over 350 have been notified since 1990. PTAs increasingly involve developing countries, whether in north-south or south-south agreements. In addition, cross-regional PTAs are becoming more common.[1]

Preferential trade agreements have been provided for under Article XXIV of the GATT since its inception in 1947, raising a puzzle as to why the founders of the GATT would have wished to accommodate arrangements that are, on their face, discriminatory between members and non-members and hence in tension with the GATT's foundational non-discrimination principles, in particular the Most Favoured Nation Principle. In part, the explanation appears to be that customs unions (but not free trade areas) were viewed as analogous to a single country for trade purposes in their dealings with outside states by virtue of their common external tariff. In the immediate post-war years greater economic and political integration within western Europe had emerged as a major policy objective not only within Europe but in the U.S. and other foreign policy circles and required special accommodation within the GATT system.[2]

---

[1] See Roberto V. Fiorentino, Jo-Ann Crawford, and Christelle Toqueboeuf, "The Landscape of Regional Trade Agreements and WTO Surveillance," in Richard E. Baldwin and Patrick Low (eds.), *Multilateralizing Regionalism* (New York: Cambridge University Press, 2009).

[2] See David A. Gantz, *Regional Trade Agreements: Law, Policy, and Practice* (Durham, N.C.: Carolina Academic Press, 2009); Kerry A. Chase, "Multilateralism Compromise: The Mysterious Origins of GATT Article XXIV," (2006) 5 *World Trade Review* 1; Kyle Bagwell and Petros

However, developing countries viewed free trade areas as better suited to their interests and argued that any special dispensations for PTAs should embrace both customs unions and free trade areas. Moreover, the U.S., which was the most vigorous proponent of multilateralism, had negotiated a secret free trade agreement with Canada and sought to have this accommodated within the GATT exception for PTAs.

II. THE LEGAL FRAMEWORK FOR PREFERENTIAL TRADE AGREEMENTS UNDER THE GATT[3]

Article XXIV of the GATT sets out the key conditions that PTAs must satisfy in order to be GATT-compliant. These provisions are supplemented by the Understanding on the Interpretation of Article XXIV of the General Agreement on Tariffs and Trade 1994, which was adopted by the member countries as part of the Uruguay Round Final Act. Parties entering into PTAs must notify these agreements to the WTO under Article XXIV:7. Until 1996, GATT working parties were convened to assess the compliance of PTAs with Article XXIV. In 1996, the Committee on Regional Trade Agreements (CRTA) was created by the WTO General Council, replacing the working parties in executing this function. The CRTA is empowered to conduct a full review and make recommendations to the General Council of the WTO on compliance of a notified PTA with the requirements of Article XXIV. However, despite this broad scope of PTA review, GATT contracting parties have never in the history of the GATT reached by consensus a decision that a notified scheme is inconsistent with the multilateral rules. The second avenue for review of PTAs is through a formal complaint to the Dispute Settlement Body of the WTO, followed by the convening of a panel and then a potential appeal to the Appellate Body. However, the only case directly addressing the issue of PTA consistency with

Mavroidis (eds), *Preferential Trade Agreements: Law, Policy and Economics* (Cambridge University Press, 2011).
  [3] See generally, Joel P. Trachtman, "International Trade: Regionalism," in Guzman and Sykes (eds.), *Research Handbook on International Economic Law, supra* Chapter 2, note 2.

the GATT is *Turkey – Textiles* (discussed below). Thus, despite the rapidly growing importance of the phenomenon of PTAs, and despite substantial ambiguities in a number of the key conditions for PTAs set out in Article XXIV, there has been remarkably little guidance on the interpretation and application of these requirements either by the CRTA or the GATT/WTO dispute-settlement system.

Article XXIV:4 addresses the purpose of PTAs and their place within the multilateral trading system and provides: "The Contracting Parties recognize the desirability of increasing freedom of trade by the development, through voluntary agreements, of closer integration between the economies of the countries parties to such agreements. They also recognize that the purpose of a customs union or of a free trade area should be to facilitate trade between the constituent territories and not to raise barriers to the trade of other Contracting Parties with such territories." The Appellate Body in *Turkey – Textiles* clarified that while Article XXIV:4 does not create an operative test for the purpose of a PTA, the entire text of Article XXIV must be interpreted in light of the purposive language in paragraph 4.

Article XXIV goes on to stipulate two key requirements for PTAs: an internal requirement and an external requirement.

With respect to the internal requirement, Article XXIV:8(a) (in the case of customs unions) and Article XXIV:8(b) (in the case of free trade areas), require that duties and other restrictive regulations of commerce be eliminated with respect to "substantially all the trade" between the constituent countries. The legal meaning of "substantially all the trade" and "other restrictive regulations of commerce" has never been fully articulated or resolved by either the CRTA or GATT/WTO panels or the Appellate Body.

With respect to the external requirement, Article XXIV:5 applies slightly different standards for customs unions and FTAs, but for both forms of PTAs it is generally required that duties and other regulations of commerce on third parties should not be "higher or more restrictive" after the creation of the PTA than before. For customs unions, which entail the creation of a common external tariff, duties or other regulations of commerce must not be higher or more restrictive "on the whole" after the creation of a PTA than before. This requirement was interpreted by the Appellate Body in *Turkey – Textiles* to provide for an "economic test" of the overall effect of the customs union on third parties; however, application of such an overall economic test poses major methodological problems which remain unresolved. In contrast, the external requirement for FTAs omits the words "on the whole", indicating a measure-by-measure approach rather than an overall economic test; each FTA member must ensure that no duties or other regulations of commerce faced by third parties are higher or more restrictive than the "corresponding duties and regulations of commerce" prior to the formation of the FTA. An additional external requirement for customs unions is contained in Article XXIV:8(a)(ii). This provision requires that "substantially the same duties and other regulations of commerce are applied by each of the members of the union to the trade of territories not included in the union." However, the meaning of this standard remains unclear in GATT/WTO jurisprudence.

The Article XXIV disciplines on PTAs have been the subject of one important Appellate Body decision (the *Turkey – Textiles* case 1999),[4] which involved a complaint by India against Turkey with respect to quantitative restrictions that Turkey had imposed on imports of textiles and clothing from India. Turkey, as part of its efforts to negotiate accession to the E.U., had entered into an arrangement with the E.U. to adopt a customs union and pursuant to these arrangements had committed itself to adopt substantially the same commercial policy as the E.U. on textiles. India alleged breaches by Turkey of Article XI and XII of the GATT and Article 2.4 of the Agreement on Textiles and Clothing. Turkey pleaded by way of defence Article XXIV of the GATT, arguing that the impugned quantitative restrictions were necessary in order to form a customs union with the E.U. and that the chapeau to Article XXIV:5 asserts that the provisions of the GATT shall not prevent the formation of a customs union.

While the Appellate Body held that Article XXIV could justify certain GATT inconsistent measures, it interpreted the chapeau of Article XXIV:5 to mean that such a defence would only be available where adherence to the GATT provisions in question would "make impossible" formation of a customs union. On the facts of the case, the Appellate Body held that this test of necessity for an Article XXIV defence was not satisfied since Turkey could have adopted

---

[4] *Turkey – Restrictions on Imports of Textile and Clothing Products*, 22 October 1999, WT/DS34/R and WT/DS34/AB/R [*Turkey – Textiles* 1999].

rules of origin that precluded trans-shipment of Indian textiles through Turkey into the E.U., enabling formation of the customs union without imposing GATT inconsistent quantitative restrictions on Indian textile and clothing imports into Turkey.

Turkey – Textiles was an important case in several respects. The Appellate Body made clear that it considers the overall compatibility of PTAs with Article XXIV to be justiciable, despite prior conventional wisdom that compliance with the requirements of Article XXIV primarily entailed political judgments by the GATT/WTO Committee on Regional Trade Agreements. Moreover, the Appellate Body made clear that Article XXIV offers a possible defence to measures inconsistent with GATT provisions beyond the MFN principle in Article I:1. However, an Article XXIV defence will only be available where formation of the customs union would be impossible in the absence of the GATT inconsistent measures – a stringent standard to satisfy.

III.   THE CONTESTED CASE FOR PREFERENTIAL TRADE AGREEMENTS

The literature debating the merits and disadvantages of PTAs is well developed and wide-ranging, but contentious. Three central issues are essential to understanding the welfare effects of PTAs. The first two concern the static welfare effects of PTAs: 1) are PTAs trade-creating or trade-diverting, and 2) does the proliferation of PTA trade rules increase transaction costs and therefore inhibit trade? The third issue concerns the dynamic welfare effects of PTAs: 3) how does the formation of PTAs affect the future course of international trade liberalization?

A.   Trade Diversion or Trade Creation

The distinction between trade creation and trade diversion derives from the seminal work of Jacob Viner in his 1950 book, *The Customs Union Issue*. The distinction drawn by Viner between trade creation and trade diversion hinges on whether removal of a trade barrier through formation of a customs union shifts the source of production of a good to a lower cost producer (for trade creation) or higher cost producer (for trade diversion), based strictly on the costs of production and abstracting from costs associated with tariffs. For example, if removal of internal trade barriers shifts production in good X from domestic producers to more efficient producers in the partner countries, then this would be trade creating and beneficial for global welfare. However, if PTA creation shifts imports from more efficient producers in third countries to less efficient producers in the customs union partner, whose comparative advantage is a function of their preferential market access, then this is trade diverting and detrimental to global welfare. In the decades following Viner's classic contribution, economic models have become considerably more sophisticated, although despite these theoretical advances the net welfare impact of PTAs remains ambiguous.[5] Empirical studies have produced similarly conflicting results.[6]

B. Transaction Costs

Each PTA includes a unique set of trade rules with which importers and exporters must comply. Bhagwati likens the global web of PTAs as a "spaghetti bowl", with each additional PTA adding complexity to international trade rules and raising the transaction costs of international trade. As PTAs multiply, a single product will be subjected to different tariff rates under different PTAs; moreover, tariff treatment will hinge on compliance with each PTA's unique, and inherently arbitrary, rules of origin.[7] Other authors challenge the scale of these transaction costs as an impediment to trade, noting that producers always have the option of exporting under the MFN tariff rate, meaning that at worst the "spaghetti bowl" cannot diminish welfare beyond the original MFN starting point.[8]

---

[5] See Arvind Panagariya, "Preferential Trade Liberalization: The Traditional Theory and New Developments," (2000) 38:2 *Journal of Economic Literature* 287.

[6] See Viet D. Do and William Watson, "Economic Analysis of Regional Trade Agreements," in Lorand Bartels and Federico Ortino (eds.), *Regional Trade Agreements in the WTO Legal System* (New York: Oxford University Press, 2006).

[7] Bhagwati, *Termites in the Trading System, supra* Chapter 1, note 20.

[8] See Do and Watson, *supra* note 6.

C. Dynamic Effects: Building Blocks or Stumbling Blocks?

The dynamic effects of PTAs concern the impact of each PTA on the subsequent path of international trade liberalization, either through the expansion of PTAs or through multilateral liberalization. Bhagwati argues that in modelling the dynamic effects of PTAs, the incentives faced by three key groups of agents must be considered. First, governments of member countries, once participating in a PTA, may avoid incurring the transaction costs of further PTA expansion due to a belief that the PTA market is already large enough. Second, interest groups in member countries, especially producer interest groups, may in some cases lobby for PTA expansion, but in others will seek protection from increased competition and oppose PTA expansion. Finally, interest groups and governments of outside countries may seek entry to, or emulation of, existing PTAs.[9] There are also reasons to suspect that PTAs could stall momentum for multilateral trade liberalization. Countries with existing or potential avenues for preferential market access are likely to have weaker incentives to pursue new markets through multilateral liberalization, a view for which there appears to be some empirical evidence.[10] It is also often argued that negotiating and managing many PTAs is likely to strain the scarce economic, legal and diplomatic resources of countries, especially developing countries, and divert resources from advancing multilateral trade liberalization initiatives. Current gridlock in multilateral trade negotiations may be, in part, either a cause or an effect of the proliferation of PTAs.

D. Additional Factors

Beyond these three key issues of trade diversion, transaction costs and dynamic effects of PTAs on global trade liberalization, a number of additional arguments are frequently advanced regarding the implications of PTAs. First, it has been claimed that PTAs

---

[9]   Jagdish Bhagwati, "Regionalism and Multilateralism: An Overview," in Jaime de Melo and Arvind Panagariya (eds.), *New Dimensions in Regional Integration* (Cambridge: Cambridge University Press, 1993).

[10]   See Nuno Limao, "Preferential Trade Agreements as Stumbling Blocks for Multilateral Trade Liberalization: Evidence for the United States," (2006) 96:3 *The American Economic Review* 896.

offer the potential for deeper and broader liberalization, given that negotiations occur within or among smaller numbers of parties, often sharing common regional histories, backgrounds, and interests; however, deeper trade liberalization within PTAs may in some cases create more trade diversion than trade creation, which is not a desirable outcome from a global welfare perspective. Second, it is sometimes claimed that PTAs enable countries to advance the liberalization agenda into new issue areas, for many of the same reasons that may motivate deeper liberalization with respect to existing impediments to trade, and in this respect PTAs may function as laboratories of integration, serving as an example or a pathfinder for future multilateral disciplines.[11] Third, it may be argued that PTAs enable the advancement of important regional and domestic political objectives that are not directly trade related, such as greater political and economic integration in western Europe as a strategy for mitigating the risk of recurrence of the massive military conflicts that devastated Europe in the first half of the twentieth century. Fourth, on the negative side of the balance sheet, it is often pointed out that PTAs often group countries with significant disparities in wealth and political influence, and that these asymmetries between parties to a PTA can generate inequitable or inefficient outcomes, in contrast to the multilateral system where at least in principle decisions are made on a consensus basis, with one country-one vote, and the potential for coalition formation in negotiations within the multilateral system that may mitigate power asymmetries.

IV. CONCLUSION

The proliferation of PTAs in the global trading system is an empirical fact, but their economic impact, political implications, and legal status are contested. The legal disciplines on PTAs under Article XXIV are poorly defined, and the relative absence of GATT/WTO jurisprudence on PTAs is a symptom of the reluctance of WTO members to enforce the disciplines of Article XXIV, given that nearly all members are now party to a PTA and bear some risk if restrictive

---

[11] See Arie Reich, "Bilateralism versus Multilateralism in International Economic Law: Applying the Principle of Subsidiarity," (2010) 60:2 *University of Toronto Law Journal* 263.

disciplines on PTAs are articulated by WTO panels or the Appellate Body. The consistency of PTAs with the multilateral trading system economically, politically, and legally is likely to constitute one of the most important and enduring challenges to the international trading system in the years ahead.

5. The National Treatment Principle

I. INTRODUCTION

A. History

The National Treatment Principle has an ancient genesis in international trade law, arguably dating back to ancient Hebrew law and then appearing in agreements between Italian city-states in the eleventh century, in commercial treaties concluded during the twelfth century between England and continental powers and cities, and in agreements among German city-states constituting the Hanseatic League from the twelfth century onwards. The principle was also adopted in various shipping treaties entered into between European powers in the seventeenth and eighteenth centuries, and became commonplace in trade treaties drawn up in large numbers in the latter part of the nineteenth century.

B. The Text of Article III of the GATT

(1) The contracting parties recognize that internal taxes and other internal charges, and laws, regulations and requirements affecting the internal sale, offering for sale, purchase, transportation, distribution or use of products in specified amounts or proportions, should not be applied to imported or domestic products so as to afford protection to domestic production.

(2) The products of the territory of any contracting party imported into the territory of any other contracting party shall not be subject, directly or indirectly, to internal taxes or other internal charges of any kind in excess of those applied, directly or indirectly, to like domestic products. Moreover, no contracting party shall otherwise apply internal taxes or other internal charges to imported or domestic products in a manner contrary to the principles set forth in paragraph 1.*

(4) The products of the territory of any contracting party imported into the territory of any other contracting party shall be accorded

treatment no less favourable than that accorded to like products of national origin in respect of all laws, regulations and requirements affecting their internal sale, offering for sale, purchase, transportation, distribution or use. The provisions of this paragraph shall not prevent the application of differential internal transportation charges which are based exclusively on the economic operation of the means of transport and not on the nationality of the product.

*A tax conforming to the requirements of the first sentence of paragraph 2 would be considered to be inconsistent with the provisions of the second sentence only in cases where competition was involved between, on the one hand, the taxed product and, on the other hand, a directly competitive or substitutable product which was not similarly taxed (Ad Note).

C. Interpretation of Article III

Over the history of the GATT/WTO, divergent approaches to the interpretation of Article III have been adopted, ranging from literalist or formalistic approaches; aims-and-effects approaches that focus on discerning protectionist intent; and economic or market-based approaches that focus on domestic fiscal or regulatory measures that upset competitive relationships between imports and domestic products.

II. THE GATT (PRE-WTO) CASE LAW

A. Internal Taxes (Article III (2))

The first *Japanese-Alcohol Beverage* case (1987)[1] was the leading GATT case on internal taxes, and in interpreting the phrase "like products" in Article III (2) tended to focus on actual or potential substitutability between imported or domestic products on the part of consumers, as well as major differences in physical characteristics. This Panel adopted the criteria proposed by the GATT Working Party on Border Tax Adjustments in 1970, which emphasized (i) product end-uses; (ii) consumers' tastes and habits; (iii) the products' properties, nature, and quality, to which later panels added a

---

[1] *Japan – Customs Duties, Taxes and Labelling Practices on Imported Wines and Alcoholic Beverages*, adopted 10 November 1987, BISD 34S/83 [*Japan – Alcoholic Beverages* 1987].

fourth criterion, that is, common customs classifications. The other notable GATT Panel decision on internal taxes was *U.S. – Taxes on Automobiles* in 1994[2] – an unadopted GATT Panel decision relating to gas guzzler and luxury excise taxes imposed by the U.S. government on domestic and imported automobiles. Foreign exporters argued that this tax had a disparate impact on them, because of their different fleet composition. In this case the GATT Panel attached some weight to the "aims-and-effects" of the legislation in question and concluded that it was not motivated by protectionism and hence was not at variance with the objective of Article III, set out in Article III (1), which is to constrain the application of domestic measures "so as to afford protection to domestic production."

B. Regulatory Measures (Article III(4))

The first major GATT Panel decision was the *U.S. – Section 337 Tariff Act* case in 1989,[3] which related to special enforcement measures against allegedly patent-infringing imports. The Panel focused on the requirement in Article III(4) that, with respect to domestic legal and regulatory measures, imports of like products be treated "no less favourably" than domestic "like products". The Panel interpreted this requirement as prescribing "effective equality of competitive opportunities" for imports and domestic like products, which the measures in question were held to infringe. This decision has been followed in this respect by later GATT/WTO decisions.

The next important GATT Panel decision on Article III(4) was the *U.S. – Tuna* case in 1991,[4] involving a U.S. ban on imported tuna caught in ways that endangered dolphins. The GATT Panel in this case held that this ban violated Article XI and required justification under Article XX and also held that the measures in question could not be considered under Article III as they did not relate to tuna as a product, but rather the methods by which tuna was caught (implying that PPMs were not a legitimate basis for distinguishing between

---

[2] *United States – Taxes on Automobiles*, 29 September 1994, unadopted, DS31/R, 1-124 [*US – Taxes on Automobiles* 1994].

[3] *United States – Section 337 of the Tariff Act of 1930*, adopted on 7 November 1989, L/6439 – 36S/345 [*US – Section 337 Tariff Act* 1989].

[4] *United States – Restrictions on Imports of Tuna*, 3 September 1991, unadopted, DS21/R BISD 39S/155 [*US – Tuna* 1991].

foreign and domestic products). This Panel decision was also not adopted by the GATT membership. Another important case was the *U.S. – Malt Beverages* case in 1992[5] involving various U.S. state fiscal and regulatory measures relating to wine and beer. With respect to various restrictions on the sale, distribution and marketing of high alcohol content beer, a Canadian complaint that these discriminated against Canadian imports was rejected on the grounds that the measures in question applied equally to domestic and foreign production and that the aims-and-effects of these measures were not protectionist but related to various health objectives.

III.   WTO (POST-1995) CASE LAW

A.   Internal Taxes

The first major case was the second *Japanese – Alcohol* case in 1996.[6] In this case both the Panel and the Appellate Body rejected the aims-and-effects test in the context of various fiscal measures that the European Union alleged discriminated against their alcohol exports to Japan. The Appellate Body held that the concept of "like product" meant different things in different GATT provisions, and invoked the analogy of an accordion that could be squeezed more widely or more narrowly depending on context. Both the Panel and the Appellate Body emphasized a market place test of "likeness" and (Article III(1)) held that the second sentence of Article III(2), dealing with internal fiscal measures required an examination of the "design, architecture, and revealing structure" of the measures in question, in determining whether they had been adopted or applied so as to afford protection to domestic products (as required by Article III(1)) – a kind of objective test of legislative intention. The Appellate Body also emphasized that Article III is not limited in its purpose to pre-

---

    [5]   *United States – Measures Affecting Alcoholic and Malt Beverages*, adopted 19 June 1992, DS23/R BISD 39S/206 [*US – Malt Beverages* 1992].
    [6]   *Japan – Taxes on Alcoholic Beverages*, 11 July 1996, WT/DS8/R, WT/DS10/R and WT/DS11/R; *Japan – Taxes on Alcoholic Beverages*, 4 October 1996, WT/DS8/AB/R, WT/DS10/AB/R, WT/DS11/AB/R [*Japan – Alcohol* 1996].

venting the undermining of prior bound tariff concessions by the adoption of subsequent protectionist domestic measures, but also applied where no tariff bindings existed.

In *Canada – Split Run Periodicals* (1997),[7] the Appellate Body overruled the Panel's finding on like products, deciding that in the context of an 80 per cent excise tax on advertising content in foreign split-run periodicals, foreign split-run periodicals and domestic non-split run periodicals were not like products. However, the Appellate Body held that they fell within the ambit of the second sentence of Article III(2), and were competitive or directly substitutable products.

In *Korea – Taxes on Alcoholic Beverages* (1998),[8] the Panel and the Appellate Body largely followed the earlier decision in the second *Japanese Alcohol* case, and adopted a market-based test of likeness, and a *de minimus* test for "similarly taxed" under Article III(2) second sentence.

In *Chile – Taxes on Alcoholic Beverages* (1999),[9] the Panel adopted a consumer utility theory approach to deciding whether Pisco and various imported liquors were like products, using the analogy of butter and margarine to illustrate the point that differences in physical characteristics do not necessarily render products unlike if they serve similar functions in the utility function of consumers. A rather similar approach was taken by the Panel in *Indonesia – Autos* (1998),[10] where differences in treatment for internal tax purposes of certain domestically produced cars and various imported cars and car components were treated as violating Article III(2), again largely on grounds relating to the high degree of substitutability by consumers amongst these products.

---

[7] *Canada – Certain Measures Concerning Periodicals*, 30 June 1997, WT/DS31/AB/R [*Canada – Split Run Periodicals* 1997].

[8] *Korea – Taxes on Alcoholic Beverages*, 17 September 1998, WT/DS75/R and WT/DS84/R; *Korea – Taxes on Alcoholic Beverages*, 18 January 1999, WT/DS75/AB/R and WT/DS84/AB/R [*Korea – Taxes on Alcoholic Beverages* 1998].

[9] *Chile – Taxes on Alcoholic Beverages*, 15 June 1999, WT/DS87/R and WT/DS110/R [*Chile – Taxes on Alcoholic Beverages* 1999].

[10] *Indonesia – Autos* 1998, *supra* Chapter 3, note 3.

B.   Regulatory Measures

In the first Appellate Body decision under the new dispute settlement regime: *U.S.–Reformulated Gasoline* (1996),[11] different treatment of U.S. and foreign refiners of gasoline in terms of base-line standards adopted for pollution abatement was held to violate Article III(4). There was no dispute that the products were like products. The Appellate Body held that the argument by the U.S. that it faced greater administrative difficulties applying the domestic measures in question to foreign refiners was not a sufficient justification for less favourable treatment under Article XX.

In *Korea – Beef* (2000),[12] where Korea had adopted a dual retailing system for domestic and imported beef, the Appellate Body held that formal differences in the way imports and domestic like products were treated were not in themselves sufficient to render the different treatment illegal under Article III(4), but some examination of disparate impacts was required, which the Appellate Body held that the Korean measures engendered.

In *E.C. – Asbestos* (2000),[13] probably the most important decision of the Appellate Body on Article III(4), the Appellate Body overruled findings by the Panel that asbestos fibres and asbestos-fibre products were "like products" relative to PCG Fibres, in the light of a French ban against the former but not the latter. While the Panel had upheld the measures under Article XX(b), the Appellate Body held that there was no violation in the first place of Article III(4). In the Appellate Body's view, all four criteria that had been adopted in prior Appellate Body and Panel decisions, largely based on the criteria proposed in the GATT Working Party Report on Border Tax Adjustments in 1970, had to be examined in order to reach an

---

[11]   *United States – Standards for Reformulated and Conventional Gasoline*, 29 January 1996, WT/DS2/R [*US – Reformulated Gasoline* 1996], as modified by the Appellate Body Report, adopted 20 May 1996, WT/DS2/AB/R.

[12]   *Korea – Measures Affecting Imports of Fresh, Chilled and Frozen Beef*, 11 December 2000, WT/DS161/AB/R and WT/DS169/AB/R [*Korea – Beef* 2000].

[13]   *European Communities – Measures Affecting Asbestos and Asbestos-Containing Products*, adopted 5 April 2001, WT/DS135/R and Add. 1, as modified by the Appellate Body Report, *European Communities – Measures Affecting Asbestos and Asbestos-Containing Products*, adopted 5 April 2001, WT/DS135/AB/R.

overall judgment on likeness. It held that the Panel had looked only at end-uses, and then only at a small number of overlapping end-uses without examining non-overlapping end-uses. The Appellate Body continued to emphasize, as it had in the second *Japanese – Alcohol*[14] case, the essentially economic test for likeness under Article III, with its focus on competitive relationships, but was of the view that there was a very heavy burden of proof on a complainant to demonstrate likeness in contexts where there were sharp differences in physical characteristics, particularly physical characteristics that related to health effects.

IV. CRITIQUE OF GATT/WTO CASE LAW

A. A Literalist/Formalistic Approach

This approach seems to have very little to recommend it in that comparing and contrasting physical characteristics, without having some purpose or rationale in mind for the comparisons is likely to be hopelessly indeterminate (in effect a "smell" test).

B. The Aims-and-Effects Approach

Both the Panel and the Appellate Body in the second *Japanese – Alcohol* case emphasized the indeterminacy of an approach that focuses on the subjective intent of legislators and regulators, often operating with very mixed motives (e.g., Baptist-bootlegger coalitions). However, the Appellate Body appears to have adopted something like an objective test of legislative intention in the second *Japanese – Alcohol*[15] case.

C. An Economic Approach

An economic approach would emphasize that whether the products are like or not is an empirical question involving an evaluation of the actual cross-elasticity of demand on the part of consumers vis-à-vis

---

[14] *Japan – Alcohol* 1996, *supra* note 6.
[15] *Japan – Alcohol* 1996, *supra* note 6.

the products in question, as is conventionally undertaken in determining relevant product markets in antitrust law. As to whether imported products have been treated less favourably than domestic products, one might also adopt from antitrust law a "raising rivals costs" approach in determining whether the measures in question have imposed greater costs on foreign producers relative to domestic producers. Under this approach differential treatment relating to health and environmental effects would require justification by the respondent under Article XX, on the theory that the respondent has better information than the complainant as to purported non-trade justifications for trade restrictive measures.[16]

D. Residual Problems

A number of difficult residual problems remain unresolved in GATT/WTO case-law interpreting and applying the National Treatment Principle.

How should one approach the question of domestic measures that distinguish between foreign and domestic products on the basis of differences in production and processing methods (PPMs)? What if these measures are imposed on both domestic and foreign products equally? What if these measures are imposed on domestic and foreign products sequentially? What if domestic measures do not relate either to product characteristics or to production and processing methods, but rather background differences in conditions in foreign and domestic countries, for example human rights abuses? What scope is there for permitting incidental adverse impacts on imports from a non-protectionist domestic measure? Finally, how should one resolve the relationship between Article III and Article XX in terms of a) the burden of proof; b) the scope of GATT exceptions?

---

[16] See Michael J. Trebilcock and Shiva K. Giri, "The National Treatment Principle in International Trade Law," in E. Kwan Choi and James C. Hartigan (eds.), *Handbook of International Trade*, Volume 2 (Blackwell Publishing, 2005).

6. Antidumping laws

I. INTRODUCTION

Antidumping laws are by far the most widely invoked of a trilogy of trade remedy or contingent protection regimes: antidumping laws; countervailing duties; and safeguards.[1] While Article VI of the GATT permitted member countries to impose antidumping laws from the outset of the GATT, up until the late 1970s antidumping laws were a relatively minor form of trade restriction, mostly because the bulk of protection was ensured by tariffs, quantitative restrictions (or voluntary export restraints), subsidies, or a mix of all these instruments. However, starting from the late 1970s both the total number of antidumping investigations and antidumping orders, as well as the number of countries that have introduced antidumping regimes have dramatically increased. As of July 2006, 1875 antidumping orders were in force around the world.[2] In many respects, it has become the protectionist remedy of choice.

India, followed by the U.S. were the leading initiators of antidumping proceedings over the period 1995 to 2006 (a total of 2938 initiations by all countries), in contrast to the period 1980 to 1988 when the actions of the U.S., Australia, Canada, and the E.U. accounted for 97.5 per cent of all actions.

---

[1] See generally, Alan O. Sykes, "International Trade: Trade Remedies," in Guzman and Sykes (eds.), *Research Handbook on International Economic Law, supra* Chapter 2, note 2; Petros C. Mavroidis, Patrick A. Messerlin and Jasper M. Wauters, *The Law and Economics of Contingent Protection in the WTO* (Cheltenham, UK: Edward Elgar, 2008).

[2] *Ibid* Chapter 1.

II. GATT/WTO PROVISIONS ON ANTIDUMPING

Article VI authorizes member countries to introduce antidumping regimes to address cases where the products of one country are introduced into the commerce of another country at less than the normal value of the products where this causes or threatens material injury to an established industry in the territory of a contracting party or materially retards the establishment of a domestic industry producing like products. A product is to be considered as being introduced into the commerce of an importing country at less than its normal value if the price at which the product is exported from one country to another a) is less than the comparable price, in the ordinary course of trade, for the like product when destined for consumption in the exporting country, or b) in the absence of such domestic price, is less than either 1) the highest comparable price for the like product for export to any third country in the ordinary course of trade, or 2) the cost of production of the product in the country of origin plus a reasonable addition for selling costs and profit. Thus, under 1) export prices are compared with prices at the same level of trade in the country of origin, while under 2), the principal comparison is between the export prices and cost of production in the country of origin (often referred to as the "constructed cost" measure). Where these conditions are met, the importing country may levy on any dumped product an antidumping duty not greater in amount than the margin of dumping in respect of such products, where the margin of dumping is the price difference determined by comparisons between the export price and either of the two country-of-origin measures noted above.

These rather cursory provisions left open many ambiguities surrounding the determination of the relevant price comparators, the concept of injury, the concept of causation, the definition of like products, and the definition of a domestic industry. In the course of the Kennedy Round that closed in the late 1960s, the Tokyo Round that closed in the late 1970s, and the Uruguay Round that closed in 1993, a much more detailed antidumping agreement has been elaborated that attempts to provide more detailed specifications of all of these key concepts. Article 2.1 of the Uruguay Round Anti-Dumping Agreement defines products as being dumped – that is, introduced into the commerce of another country at less than their normal value

– if the export price is less than the comparable price, in the ordinary course of trade, for the like product when destined for consumption in the exporting country. Where there are no sales of the like product in the ordinary course of trade in the domestic market of the exporting country, or when because of the particular market situation or the low volume of sales in the domestic market of the exporting country (a sufficient quantity must normally constitute five per cent or more of the sales of the product to the importing country) such sales do not permit a proper comparison, the margin of dumping shall be determined by comparison with a comparable price of the like product when exported to an appropriate third country, or with the cost or production in the country of origin plus a reasonable amount for administrative, selling and general costs, and for profits. Sales in the domestic market of the exporting country below per unit (fixed and variable) costs of production plus administrative, selling and general costs, may be disregarded in determining normal value if made for an extended period of time (normally one year) in substantial quantities (more than 20 per cent of transactions). Thus, all export sales, whether above or below total costs, will be averaged to obtain the export price, while generally only domestic sales above total costs will be averaged (increasing the likelihood of a finding of dumping). Where there are no home market or third country sales on which to base price comparisons, constructed value may be used, which includes materials and labour costs and an amount for selling, general and administrative expenses (SG and A) plus profit. These latter costs – SG and A and profit – must now generally be based on actual data pertaining to production and sales in the ordinary course of business by the exporter (Article 2.2).

Comparison between the export price and the normal value should be "fair" as stipulated under Article 2.4, which provides that the existence of margins of dumping shall normally be established on the basis of a comparison of weighted average domestic sale prices and weighted average export market prices, or by a comparison of domestic prices and export prices on a transaction-to-transaction basis. This precludes comparing isolated low priced export transactions with weighted average domestic prices to establish dumping.

Under Article 3, determination of injury for purposes of Article VI of GATT 1994 shall be based on positive evidence and involve an objective examination of both a) the volume of the dumped imports and the effect of the dumped imports on prices in the domestic market for like products, and b) the consequent impact of these imports on domestic producers of such products. Where imports of a product from more than one country are simultaneously subject to antidumping investigations, the investigating authorities may cumulatively assess the effects of such imports if they exceed certain *de minimus* thresholds. The examination of the impact of the dumped imports on the domestic industry concerned shall include an evaluation of all relevant economic factors having a bearing on the state of the industry (which are enumerated in Article 3.4). The authorities shall also examine any known factors other than the dumped imports, which at the same time are injuring the domestic industry, and the injuries caused by these other factors must not be attributed to the dumped imports. A determination of the threat of material injury shall be based on facts and not merely on allegation, conjecture or remote possibility. The change in circumstances which would create a situation in which the dumping would cause injury must be clearly foreseen and imminent.

Under Article 5.8, investigations shall be terminated when a dumping margin is *de minimus* (less than two per cent of the normal value) or when the volume of dumped products is negligible (i.e., if the volume of dumped imports from a particular country accounts for less than three per cent of imports of the like product in the importing country, unless countries that individually account for less than three per cent of imports collectively account for more than seven per cent of imports).

Under Article 7, provisional measures may be applied if an investigation has been initiated and a preliminary affirmative determination has been made of dumping and injury to a domestic industry. Provisional measures may take the form of a provisional duty or a security (a cash deposit or bond) equal to the amount of the antidumping duties provisionally estimated.

Under Article 8, proceedings may be suspended or terminated on receipt of the satisfactory voluntary undertaking from any exporter to revise its prices or to cease exports at dumped prices. Price undertakings may not be sought or accepted unless preliminary determinations of dumping and injury have been made and, even if then sought and accepted, the exporter may elect to have the investigation completed. In the event of a negative determination, undertakings lapse.

Under Article 17.6, in dispute settlement proceedings before the WTO under the Antidumping Agreement, a WTO Panel in its assessment of the facts of the matter shall determine whether the domestic authorities' establishment of the facts was proper and whether their evaluation of those facts was unbiased and objective. If the establishment of the facts was proper and the evaluation was unbiased and objective, even though the Panel might have reached a different conclusion, the evaluation shall not be overturned. WTO Panels shall interpret the relevant provisions of the Agreement in accordance with customary rules of interpretation of public international law. Where the Panel finds that a relevant provision of the Agreement admits of more than one permissible interpretation, the Panel shall find the domestic authorities' measures to be in conformity with the Agreement if it rests upon one of those permissible interpretations.

Despite these attempts at a greater specification of key requirements for the imposition of antidumping duties, in recent years formal trade disputes over the imposition of antidumping duties by member countries have accounted for a substantial part of the workload of WTO Panels and the Appellate Body. Between 1995 and the end of 2007, Leitner and Lester report 72 formal complaints relating to the application of antidumping measures, exceeded only by complaints relating to general GATT provisions and complaints relating to the Subsidies and Countervailing Measures Agreement.[3] Many of these disputes have related to the determinations of the two price or cost comparisons noted above. For example, the practice of the U.S. and the E.U. of attaching zero weight in determining country of origin prices to prices that entail negative dumping margins ("zeroing") – home market prices lower than export market prices – have been repeatedly challenged before WTO Panels and the Appellate Body, and have been repeatedly found non-compliant,[4] although the U.S. continues to insist, as one of its key negotiating positions, that such a practice be recognized in the course of the current Doha Round negotiations.

In addition, in two dispute-settlement proceedings, the remedies applied by the U.S., once an affirmative determination of dumping, material injury, and causation has been made, have also

---

[3] Leitner and Lester, *supra* Chapter 2, note 3 at 184.
[4] Most definitely by the Appellate Body in *U.S. – Continued Existence and Application of Zeroing Methodology*, as modified by the Appellate Body report WT/DS350/AB/R, 11 February 2009.

been challenged in recent dispute-settlement proceedings. In the *U.S. – Antidumping Act 1916* in 2000,[5] the Appellate Body held that the treble damages complainants were authorized to recover under this Act for injury caused by dumping were not one of the three authorized remedies for dumping under the WTO Antidumping Agreement, that is, provisional duties, price undertakings, or definitive duties. Similarly, in the *U.S. – Continued Dumping and Subsidy Offset Act* of 2000[6] (often referred to as the Byrd Amendment), the Appellate Body held that an amendment to U.S. antidumping legislation that required antidumping duties to be distributed to members of the injured domestic industry was non-compliant with the WTO Antidumping Agreement on similar grounds. Subsequent arbitration proceedings were brought under Article 22.6 of the Dispute Settlement Understanding as to the scale of the trade retaliation that many of the complainant countries in these proceedings were authorized to impose on the U.S., given its continuing failure to bring its antidumping laws into compliance with the Appellate Body's decision. These revealed a new set of complexities in determining the equivalence of trade sanctions to the adverse trade effects caused to these complainants by the distribution of antidumping duties to members of the domestic U.S. industries in question.

III. DOMESTIC ADMINISTRATION OF ANTIDUMPING DUTIES

In Canada and the U.S., a similar bifurcated determination process is employed. The determination of whether dumping is occurring and what the margin of dumping is are decided, in the case of Canada, by Revenue Canada, and in the case of the U.S. by the International Trade Administration of the Department of Commerce. Material injury determinations, in the case of Canada, are made by the Canadian International Trade Tribunal, and in the case of the U.S., by the International Trade Commission, both specialized

---

[5] *United States – Anti-Dumping Act of 1916*, WT/DS136, D162/AB/R (00-3369), adopted by the Dispute Settlement Body, 26 September 2000 [*US 1916* 2000].

[6] *US – Continued Dumping and Subsidy Offset Act* 2000, WT/DS217/AB/R and WT/DS234/AB/R [*US Byrd Amendment* 2000].

administrative agencies that typically hold elaborate hearings and review large bodies of documentary and oral evidence in the course of reaching their determinations. In the case of the European Union, the European Commission makes both of these sets of determinations in a much less public or transparent process than that which obtains in Canada and the U.S., subject to appeals to the European General Court and ultimately the European Court of Justice, which have been typically deferential to the European Commission.

In terms of the substantive issues to be resolved in domestic antidumping proceedings, the key issues are as follows.

A. The Dumping Determination

This entails estimating the normal value of the goods by reference to country-of-origin prices, constructed costs, or surrogate third country export prices in the case of transition economies and comparing this normal value with export prices in the country of importation. This comparison in turn yields the margin of dumping.

B. Injury Determination

The injury determination requires an evaluation of the impact of dumping on the domestic producers of a majority of like products. Indicators of material injury, according to Article 3.4 of the Uruguay Round Antidumping Agreement, can include a variety of factors, such as actual and potential decline in sales, profits, output, market share, productivity, return on investments, or utilization of capacity; factors affecting domestic prices; the magnitude of the margin of dumping; actual and potential negative effects on cash flow, inventories, employment, wages, growth, ability to raise capital or investments.

C. Causation

Under Article 3.5 of the Antidumping Agreement it must be demonstrated that the dumped imports are, through the effects of dumping, causing injury within the meaning of this Agreement. The demonstration of a causal relationship between the dumped imports and the injury to the domestic industry must be based on an examination of all relevant evidence before the authorities. The authorities must also examine any known factors other than the dumped imports which at the same time are injuring the domestic industry, and the injuries caused by these other factors must not be attributed to the dumped imports (a non-attribution requirement).

Causation has been a source of persistent controversy in domestic antidumping proceedings, in WTO dispute-settlement proceedings, and in the scholarly literature. The generally prevailing approach in the U.S. and many other countries is to adopt a bifurcated approach to the determination of the causation issue by, on the one hand, determining the existence of dumping and the margin of dumping, while on the other hand looking at trends over some recent representative period, for example three years, relating to the condition of the domestic industry. If the volume of dumped imports or the margin of dumping has been increasing, while the financial condition of the domestic industry, in various dimensions, has been declining, causation will typically simply be inferred. This technique essentially equates correlation with causation, and has been trenchantly criticized by law and economics scholars on that account.[7]

An alternative approach that is more economically defensible is the so-called unified or integrated approach where one asks what the condition of the domestic industry would be if dumping had not been occurring. This approach typically involves constructing a counter-factual where the price of imports is hypothetically raised so as to eliminate any margin of dumping, and then in the light of estimates of elasticities of domestic supply and demand and foreign supply, one reaches some judgement about the relative condition of the domestic industry with dumping and without dumping. This approach, for example, rules out attributing causation of material injury to dumped imports where the margin of dumping may be very small and where the domestic industry is really simply complaining about low-priced imports (whether dumped or not), and opportunistically seizes onto the fact that some small margin of dumping can be demonstrated.

Canadian antidumping law, contained in the Special Import

[7] See Ronald Cass and Michael Kroll, "The Economics of 'Injury' in Antidumping and Countervailing Duty Cases: A Reply to Professor Sykes," in J.S. Bhandari and Alan O. Sykes (eds.), *Economic Dimensions in International Law: Comparative and Empirical Perspectives* (Cambridge University Press, 1997).

Measures Act, contains an unusual provision authorizing the Canadian International Trade Tribunal (CITT), after making the foregoing determinations, to hold a public interest hearing to determine whether imposing antidumping duties would be contrary to the public interest, despite the fact that they meet all of the foregoing conditions. The Tribunal reports to the Minister of Finance who has discretion to lower or remove the duty. A prominent example of the exercise of this discretion is a 1998 case in which Revenue Canada found dumping of prepared baby food by Gerber U.S. and the CITT found material injury to the only other supplier of baby food in Canada, Heinz Canada. The public controversy that resulted when Gerber left the Canadian market led the CITT to hold a public interest hearing and to recommend that 60 per cent antidumping duties be reduced by approximately two-thirds due to concerns about the impact of price increases on low income families, lack of consumer choice, security of supply, rates of innovation and quality of service with only one supplier to the Canadian market. Despite the implementation of this reduction, Gerber did not return to the market. Following the five-year expiry review mandated by the WTO Antidumping Agreement to determine whether material injury to the domestic industry was likely to result from an expiry, the CITT in 2003 refused to extend the duties, finding that any injury that Heinz might suffer from Gerber's re-entry into the Canadian market would be due, for the most part, to the effects of renewed competition into the market, not to dumping.[8]

D. Chapter 19 NAFTA Binational Panel Reviews

One of Canada's principal negotiating objectives in entering into negotiations for a Canada–U.S. Free Trade Agreement in the mid-1980s was to secure relief against harassment of Canadian exports under U.S. trade remedy laws.

The result of these negotiations was that under Chapter 19 of the Canada–U.S. Free Trade Agreement of 1988 and Chapter 19 of NAFTA, which largely superseded it in 1993, binational panel reviews of domestic antidumping and countervailing duty

---

[8] See Michael Trebilcock and Andrew Tepperman, "The CITT's Baby Foods Decision: Evaluating Dumping-Related Injury When the Domestic Producer is a Monopolist," (Fall 2004) *The Competition Policy Record* 38.

determinations have been instituted. Panels of five adjudicators drawn from the two countries involved in the antidumping proceedings are authorized to review determinations by domestic agencies on dumping issues, in accordance with the legal standard of review obtaining in the respondent country before domestic courts reviewing decisions of such agencies. Where the Panel finds deficiencies in these determinations, it remands the issues back to the domestic agency for redetermination. This process of binational panel review has been widely utilized since it was first introduced under the Canada–U.S. Free Trade Agreement in 1988. Indeed, most Canada–U.S. antidumping determinations have led to the initiation of binational panel review proceedings, in turn resulting in a strikingly high remand rate.

IV. NORMATIVE RATIONALES FOR ANTIDUMPING DUTIES

A. Economic Rationales[9]

1. Price discrimination
In a typical dumping case, foreign exporters charge less for their goods in export markets than they charge in their country of origin, despite the fact that presumably selling in export markets involves some additional costs, such as transportation. These price discrepancies may be explained by a number of factors, including the fact that the foreign exporter may have a more firmly established reputation in its own domestic market and hence be able to sustain higher prices than when it is attempting to establish a presence in foreign markets for the first time; the foreign exporter's domestic market may be regulated in such a fashion or be subject to such weak or ineffective competition laws that the foreign exporter has some degree of market power in its own domestic market; or its own domestic market position may be protected by trade barriers of one kind or another. Hence, the foreign exporter may face more intense competition in export markets than in its home market. Domestic

---

[9] For an excellent treatment of these rationales, see Mavroidis, Messerlin, and Wauters, *supra* note 1.

price discrimination is often prohibited under domestic competition or antitrust laws, in a limited range of circumstances, although the Canadian Competition Act has recently been amended to remove this prohibition from the Act. Domestic price discrimination is ubiquitous, for example, airlines, movie theatres, telephone calls, and so on. Most competition/antitrust law specialists generally regard the case for constraints on domestic price discrimination as dubious at best, as price discrimination tends to raise output toward competitive levels. However, whatever the merits of disciplining domestic price discrimination, the case for disciplining international price discrimination (such as antidumping often entails) is even weaker, in that geographic price discrimination that yields both high-priced and low-priced markets (depending on differences in demand elasticities) in the case of international price discrimination yields a low-priced market in the importing country and a high-priced market in the exporting country, which would seem of little or no concern to importing countries that benefit from the lower-priced imports.

2. Predation

Under many countries' domestic competition or antitrust laws, predatory pricing is either prohibited on a stand-alone basis or is viewed as symptomatic of abuse of dominance. In most cases of predatory pricing, a dominant firm, in the face of price competition from rivals, may cut its prices below its costs, incurring a loss in the short-run, with a view to driving actual or potential rivals out of the market, and then raising prices subsequently to supra-competitive or monopolistic levels, enabling it to recoup any short-run losses and make monopoly profits in the longer term. As with price discrimination, most competition/antitrust law specialists regard anti-competitive forms of domestic predation as a relatively rare occurrence, largely because it is likely to prove an unsuccessful or at least highly risky strategy, given the certainty of short-run losses and the uncertainty of future monopoly profits in the face of the prospect of future competitive entry. However, even amongst those commentators who believe that a domestic anti-predation law is warranted, it is widely accepted that it is generally symptomatic of abuse of a dominant position in the market. In the case of international dumping, where historically most antidumping actions have been brought by major importers, often against exporters in smaller countries, it seems totally implausible to assume that the foreign exporters could realistically aspire to monopolizing the importing country's market. One illustrative case is the antidumping complaint brought in Canada by General Motors and Ford against Hyundai for allegedly selling cars in Canada in the mid-1980s, at the time it was first entering the Canadian market, at 36 per cent less than it sold them for in South Korea. It is not seriously arguable that Hyundai was using supra-competitive profits garnered in its protected South Korean market to finance below-cost exports to the Canadian market, where it held a market share of 2 or 3 per cent, with a view to predating (monopolizing) the latter market.[10] Moreover, a study by Hutton and Trebilcock of the 30 cases between 1984 and 1989 in which Canada imposed antidumping duties found that none could be supported on predatory pricing grounds.[11] An unpublished study for the OECD of a much larger sample of antidumping cases apparently reached similar conclusions.[12]

3. Intermittent dumping

Jacob Viner, in an early economic analysis of dumping, was concerned that some dumping could be characterized as intermittent, reflecting gluts or surpluses of, for example perishable agricultural products in exporting countries, but as not reflecting a sustainable source of supply, while arguably disrupting more efficient domestic industries, and hence leading to higher costs for consumers in the long run.[13] While Viner may have been correct that intermittent dumping is inefficient in that it reduces total social welfare in the importing country, the concern seems applicable to a very narrow range of circumstances and moreover is not an explicit focus of domestic antidumping proceedings. Indeed, Hutton and Trebilcock find that the only Canadian antidumping cases of the 30 that they analyzed in detail that exhibited any indication of intermittent dumping were a handful of cases involving agricultural imports.

---

[10]   Mathew Kronby, "Kicking the Tires," (1991) 18 *Canadian Business L.J.* 95.
[11]   Susan Hutton and Michael Trebilcock, "An Empirical Study of the Application of Canadian Antidumping Laws: A Search for Normative Rationales," (1990) 24 *Journal of World Trade* 123.
[12]   See "Attack on Antidumping Laws Sparks OECD Row," *Financial Times*, 21 September 1995.
[13]   See Jacob Viner, *Dumping: A Problem in International Trade* (University of Chicago Press, 1933).

B. Non-economic Rationales

1. Distributive justice

It might be argued that antidumping duties serve to advance distributive justice goals by protecting "least advantaged" groups in importing countries (in a Rawlesian sense). These groups might include low-skilled, low-paid, immobile workers. However, the problem with this argument is that such impacts, while a perfectly legitimate source of concern, are not limited to dumped imports but any low-priced imports, dumped or not, and would seem to call for quite different policy responses than antidumping laws, including safeguard laws and other forms of domestic adjustment assistance. Moreover, Hutton and Trebilcock find that only a very small number of the 30 cases they examined seem to fit within this rationale – in many cases the workers involved in the domestic industry were better paid than average workers in Canada.

2. Communitarianism

A related concern is that the dumping laws may advance the objective of protecting long-standing communities that are dependent on particular industries and are threatened by import competition, along with the social ties and networks that are valuable to members of such communities. Again, as with distributive justice concerns, it is not obvious why this concern should be restricted to dumped imports, as opposed to low-priced imports generally (dumped or not), and again other policy responses are likely to be much more effective. Hutton and Trebilcock find very few cases in their sample of 30 cases where this concern seems legitimately engaged.

C. Political Rationales

Alan Sykes argues that rather than attempting to ascribe an economic logic to antidumping laws, it is more persuasive to view them as part of a grand political compact among major trading nations where in order to facilitate major trade liberalization concessions with respect to border measures such as tariffs and quantitative restrictions, member countries by agreement reserved to themselves various unilateral "opt-out" regimes, including antidumping duties, against the contingency that the discrete impacts of import competition in particular sectors would prove politically unsustainable. He argues that in the absence of these opt-outs or safety valves, governments would have been more reluctant to assume the political risks of trade liberalization initiatives in the first place.[14] Sykes' argument is a subtle and disconcerting one, in that it is inherently non-refutable through any decisive a priori analysis. However, it seems to assume that there is some constant quotient of protectionism in the world which needs to be preserved, so that if tariffs or other border measures are reduced other outlets need to be found for this fixed quotient of protectionism. This seems empirically a highly suspect hypothesis, given the extensive forms and degrees of trade liberalization that have occurred in the post-war years. Moreover, even if the argument is correct in its own terms, it is not clear why this justifies antidumping duties rather than a well-conceived safeguards regime.

V.   REFORMING ANTIDUMPING DUTY REGIMES

Various options are open to consideration, ranging from the modest to the ambitious. At the modest end of the spectrum, one could tinker with the existing WTO rules in various ways; for example, prohibiting "zeroing"; introducing a public interest exception as in Canadian antidumping laws; adopting a unified or integrated causation test. It is doubtful that any of these reforms would have a dramatic impact on the utilization of antidumping laws. One could also imagine strengthening the role of binational or multilateral review of the domestic application of antidumping laws, for example by giving binational panels under Chapter 19 of NAFTA dispositive power over antidumping determinations, rather than merely remand power, and perhaps creating some form of regional equivalent of the Appellate Body to replace the current Extraordinary Challenge Committees. One could also remove Article 17.6 from the Antidumping Agreement, which requires the Dispute Settlement Body to show deference to domestic agencies, both on factual determinations and in the interpretation of provisions of the Antidumping Agreement. However, again it is hard to imagine that such reforms

---

[14]   See Alan O. Sykes, "The Economics of Injury in Antidumping and Countervailing Duty Cases," (1996) 16 *International Review of Law and Economics* 5.

are likely to have a dramatic impact on the utilization of antidumping laws.

A much more ambitious reform would be to contemplate the repeal of current antidumping laws and replace them with a harmonized anti-predation law, whereby a country is authorized to enact domestic legislation (if such does not already exist) that penalizes or prohibits international forms of predatory pricing. This is likely to have a dramatic impact on the scope of antidumping laws, given the rarity of successful predation prosecutions or civil suits under domestic competition or antitrust law and would probably reduce positive antidumping determinations by upwards of 90 per cent. This is the course that has been taken by Australia and New Zealand under their regional free trade treaty, and predictably has led to the end of antidumping actions between the two countries. In this way, the National Treatment Principle would be fully respected, in that domestic and foreign producers of competitive products would be put on exactly the same footing in terms of the pricing practices in which they are permitted to engage. Current antidumping laws are flagrantly discriminatory by imposing much more stringent disciplines on the pricing behaviour of foreign producers than the pricing constraints imposed under domestic competition/antitrust laws on domestic producers. One might end with a final question: is reform along these lines remotely feasible in the future, and if not why not?

7. Subsidies and countervailing duties

I. INTRODUCTION

Allegedly trade-distorting subsidies conferred on domestic industries by member countries have been a longstanding issue of contention in trade policy circles, and according to Leitner and Lester[1] accounted for 78 issues in dispute in formal trade dispute proceedings between 1995 and 2007 – more than any other GATT/WTO agreement, other than the basic GATT itself. A number of these disputes have been high profile, including the long-running softwood lumber dispute between Canada and the U.S.; the dispute between Brazil and Canada over aircraft subsidies by both countries; the dispute between the E.U. and the U.S. over U.S. taxation of Foreign Sales Corporations; the dispute between Brazil and the U.S. over U.S. subsidies to domestic cotton production; the dispute over E.U. subsidies to sugar production; and the current dispute between the U.S. and the E.U. over subsidies to Boeing and Airbus.

It is useful to keep in mind three basic subsidy scenarios:

a. Country A subsidizes exports of products to Country B, allegedly causing material injury to domestic producers of like products in Country B. This is the classic countervailing duty scenario.
b. Country A subsidizes exports to Country C and as a result squeezes out exports from Country B to Country C's market.
c. Country A subsidizes domestic production of products for its own market, having the effect of squeezing out imports from Country B into Country A's market.

---

[1]   Leitner and Lester, *supra* Chapter 2, note 3 at 184.

The latter two scenarios do not implicate the potential imposition of unilateral countervailing duties given that the subsidized products are not moving from Country A to Country B's market, but instead raise the potential for a formal complaint under the Dispute Settlement Provisions of the WTO.

II. THE GATT SUBSIDIES REGIME

Under Article VI of the GATT, member countries may impose countervailing duties on imports into their domestic markets in an amount not in excess of the estimated bounty or subsidy determined to have been granted, directly or indirectly, on the manufacture, production, or export of such product in the country of origin or exportation. Under Article VI, as with dumping, no countervailing duties may be imposed unless there has been a determination that the effect of subsidization is such as to cause or threaten material injury to an established domestic industry, or is such as to retard materially the establishment of a domestic industry producing like products. No product should be subject to countervailing duties by reason of the exemption of such product from duties or taxes borne by the like product when destined for consumption in the country of origin, or by reason of the refund of such duties or taxes, reflecting the theory that countries of importation may well wish to impose consumption taxes on such imports and that exemption from payment of such taxes in countries of origin simply avoids double taxation. After antidumping actions, countervailing duty actions are generally the most frequently initiated type of trade remedy. Between 1995–2008, the U.S. reported the most initiations, with 88 of 217, followed by the E.U. with 48. Developed countries were responsible for 181, or 83.4 per cent of countervailing duty initiations. Developing countries were the object of the majority of initiations at 133.[2]

Under Article XVI of the GATT, if any contracting party grants or maintains any subsidy which operates directly or indirectly to increase exports of any product from, or to reduce imports of any product into, its territory, it must notify the contracting parties of

---

[2] WTO CV Initiations by Reporting Members 01/01/95–30/06/09. Available online at www.wto.org.

the nature and extent of the subsidization and of its likely effects on imports and exports and upon request discuss with other contracting parties concerned the possibility of limiting subsidization. Additional provisions were added to Article XVI in 1955 dealing with export subsidies, whereby contracting parties agreed not to grant either directly or indirectly any form of subsidy on the export of any product other than a primary product, where such a subsidy results in the sale of such a product at a price lower than the comparable price charged for the like product to buyers in the domestic market. In the case of subsidies on the export of primary products, contracting parties agreed that such subsidies should not be applied in a manner which results in the subsidizing party having more than an equitable share of world export trade in that product, taking account of the shares of the contracting parties in such trade in the product during a previous representative period. However, the consultation provisions of Article XVI have proved largely ineffectual, and the additional provisions on export subsidies were not adopted by many members of the GATT, in particular most developing country members.

During the Tokyo Round of multilateral negotiations that ended in the late 1970s a more detailed subsidies code was negotiated that attempted to set out some basic disciplines for two tracks or avenues of complaints – first, unilateral imposition of countervailing duties by member countries pursuant to domestic countervailing duty laws; and second, subsidies falling into all three of the scenarios described above could constitute the subject of a formal complaint under the Dispute Settlement provisions of the GATT which, if upheld, could eventually lead to the authorization of retaliatory trade sanctions against the country whose subsidies were held in violation of the disciplines set out in this code. However, many of the rules contained in this agreement remained vague. For example, export subsidies on primary products were subject to a rule that was not much more specific than the rule contained in Article XVI of the GATT, and disciplines on domestic subsidies were subject to a wide range of exceptions or qualifications which permitted member countries to provide such subsidies, subject only to the vague requirement that they take into account possible adverse effects on trade. Moreover, the Tokyo Round Subsidies Code was a plurilateral, not a multilateral, agreement and was adopted mostly by OECD countries and not by most developing countries.

III. THE URUGUAY ROUND SUBSIDIES AND COUNTERVAILING MEASURES (SCM) AGREEMENT

In the course of the Uruguay Round of multilateral trade negotiations that ended in December 1993, a much more detailed subsidies agreement was negotiated (henceforth the SCM Agreement). This agreement is part of the single undertaking that all members of the WTO were required to commit themselves to, and hence is a multilateral and not plurilateral agreement (in contrast to the Tokyo Round Subsidies Code). Like the Tokyo Round Code, the SCM Agreement preserves two tracks or avenues for objection to other countries' subsidies policies: the unilateral imposition of countervailing duties on subsidized imports, and the filing of a formal complaint with the WTO Dispute Settlement Body, with the possibility for the imposition of retaliatory sanctions in the event that the complaint is upheld.

The SCM Agreement essentially adopts what has been described as a red light, yellow light, and green light approach to subsidies. Under Article 3 of the SCM Agreement, two classes of subsidies are prohibited outright: a) subsidies contingent, in law or in fact, upon export performance, and b) subsidies contingent upon the use of domestic over imported goods (the red light category of subsidies). Under Article 8 of the SCM Agreement, certain subsidies are declared to be non-actionable, including certain subsidies for research and development, certain types of assistance to disadvantaged regions, and certain subsidies for compliance with environmental regulations. These green light provisions were scheduled to expire in 2000 unless renewed (Article 31), which the members have not chosen to do. This, then, focuses our attention on the intermediate or yellow light class of subsidies, deemed to be actionable subsidies under Part III of the SCM Agreement.

Article 1 of the SCM Agreement contains a fairly detailed definition of a subsidy which must entail a financial contribution by government, including direct transfers of funds (e.g., grants, loans and equity infusions), potential direct transfers of funds or liabilities (e.g., loan guarantees); government revenue otherwise due that is foregone or not collected; government provision of goods or services other than general infrastructure; government purchases of goods. In addition, a benefit must thereby be conferred by the subsidy in question.

With respect to actionable subsidies, a subsidy must also be "specific" as defined in Article 2, whereby the granting authority either explicitly or implicitly limits access to a subsidy to certain enterprises. In the case of actionable subsidies, Article 5 provides that no member shall cause, through the use of any subsidy, the following adverse effects to the interests of any other member: that is, a) injury to the domestic industry of another member; b) nullification or impairment of benefits accruing directly or indirectly to other members, in particular the benefits of tariff concessions bound under Article II of the GATT; and c) serious prejudice to the interests of another member. Serious prejudice is defined, in turn, in Article 6 as arising in any case where one or several of the following apply:

a) the effect of the subsidy is to displace or impede the imports of a like product of another member into the market of the subsidizing member;
b) the effect of the subsidy is to displace or impede the exports of a like product of another member from a third country market;
c) the effect of the subsidy is a significant price undercutting by the subsidized product as compared with the price of a like product of another member in the same market or significant price suppression, price depression, or lost sales in the same market; or
d) the effect of the subsidy is an increase in the world market share of the subsidizing member in a particular subsidized primary product or commodity as compared to the average share it had during the previous period of three years and this increase follows a consistent trend over a period when subsidies have been granted.

The SCM Agreement contains various transitional provisions that provide various dispensations to developing countries or countries in transition from command to market economies, particularly with respect to the time within which they are required to bring their subsidy practices into compliance with the provisions of the SCM Agreement. In the case of actionable subsidies, the relevant provisions in the SCM Agreement do not apply to subsidies maintained on agricultural products as provided in Article 13 of the Agreement on Agriculture (the so-called "Peace Clause", which expired at the beginning of 2004). Part 7 of the SCM Agreement sets out detailed annual reporting requirements for members with respect to actionable subsidies granted or maintained within their territories to the Committee on Subsidies and Countervailing Measures. Finally, Part V of the SCM Agreement sets out a number of detailed procedural provisions governing the unilateral imposition of countervailing measures, which broadly parallel the procedures applicable to antidumping actions.

IV. WTO CASE LAW ON THE INTERPRETATION AND APPLICATION OF SUBSIDY RULES

A substantial body of complex WTO case law (both Panel and Appellate Body decisions) has developed since 1995 on some of the key provisions in the SCM Agreement. A number of the key interpretive issues that have required resolution are briefly summarized below.

A. Subsidy

First, as to the definition of a subsidy, Article 1.1 of the SCM Agreement defines a subsidy as a financial contribution by a government or any public body within the territory of a member whereby a benefit is thereby conferred. In *E. C. – Large Civil Aircraft*,[3] the Panel discussed potential direct transfers of funds under particular loan guarantees. The Panel noted that loan guarantees benefit their recipients because they enable them to obtain for lower prices the loans guaranteed. Thus, according to the Panel, an assessment regarding potential direct transfers of funds should focus on the existence of a government practice that involves an obligation to make a direct transfer of funds which, in and of itself, is claimed to be capable of conferring a benefit on the recipient that is separate and independent from the benefit that might be conferred from any future transfer of funds. The *U. S. – FSC*[4] dispute involved a challenge by a number of countries of billions of dollars of tax exemptions given to off-shore

---

[3] *European Communities – Measures Affecting Trade in Large Civil Aircraft*, (2010) WT/DS 316/R.
[4] *United States – Fair Treatment of Foreign Sales Corporations* (2000) WT/DS108/AB/R.

"foreign sales corporations" by the United States. These corporations were typically subsidiaries of U.S.-based corporations selling goods into foreign markets. The Appellate Body was required to address the meaning of "otherwise due" in the phrase "government revenue that is otherwise due, is foregone, or not collected" in Article 1.1 of the SCM Agreement. The principal issue was whether a comparator may be found in the actions of other members or solely the member whose actions are being challenged. The Appellate Body found that "otherwise due" requires, on the basis of a normative benchmark, a comparison between revenues raised and those which would otherwise have been raised and that this benchmark varies between members according to their own tax scheme. In *U.S. – Softwood Lumber IV*,[5] the Appellate Body upheld the Panel's determination that Canadian provincial governments made "financial contributions" to timber producers by providing them with rights to harvest standing timber through government stumpage programs in return for royalties. As to the meaning of "general infrastructure" in Article 1.1, the Panel in *E.C. – Large Civil Aircraft* held that the determination of whether or not a measure involves general infrastructure must be made on a case-by-case basis, taking into account the existence of de jure or de facto limitations on access or use, and any other factors that tend to demonstrate that the infrastructure was or was not provided to or for the use of only a single entity or a limited group of entities. On the facts of this case, the Panel found that the E.C. had provided specific forms of infrastructure assistance to Airbus.

B.   Benefit

With respect to the interpretation of the phrase "benefit thereby conferred" in Article 1.1, the Appellate Body in *Canada – Aircraft*[6] affirmed the Panel's interpretation of this term that in order to confer a "benefit", a financial contribution must be provided on terms that are more advantageous than those that would have been available to the recipient on the market. This in turn raises questions of what is the relevant market comparison. In the softwood lumber

---

5   *United States – Final Countervailing Duty Determination with Respect to Certain Softwood Lumber from Canada* (2004) WT/DS257/AB/R.
6   *Canada – Measures Affecting the Export of Civil Aircraft* (1999) WT/DS70/AB/R.

dispute between Canada and the U.S., the U.S. argued that the prevailing market conditions in Canada did not reflect the fair market value of timber in Canada because of the large involvement of Canadian governments in that market. Reversing the decision of the Panel that prevailing market prices may not be disregarded simply because they are distorted, the Appellate Body held that an investigating authority may use a benchmark other than private prices in the country of provision where it has been established that private prices in that country are distorted. Other WTO cases have wrestled with the question of the effect of subsidies on state-owned enterprises once they are privatized in an arm's length transaction. In *U.S. – Countervailing Measures on Certain E.C. Products*,[7] the Appellate Body held that although there should be a presumption that a benefit no longer exists after a firm is privatized at market value in an arm's length transaction, there may be market conditions where the value of a continuing benefit from a past financial contribution to the preprivatized firm is not fairly reflected in the market price at which a new owner purchases an entity from the government.

C. Specificity

With respect to the requirement of specificity that must be satisfied in order for a subsidy to be actionable (prohibited subsidies are deemed to be specific), Article 2 of the SCM Agreement indicates that subsidies may be de jure or de facto specific, but as demonstrated in the long-running *Canada – U.S. Softwood Lumber* dispute, where U.S. authorities reached divergent findings on this issue in successive countervailing duty proceedings, how small a number of firms or industries must benefit from a subsidy in order for it to be specific has an element of arbitrariness to it, with a focus on upstream input markets yielding a smaller number of recipients on the facts of this case than a focus on the number of firms or industries involved in using softwood lumber as inputs into the production of downstream products. The decisions by the Panel and Appellate Body in *U.S. – Upland Cotton*[8] generally suggest that the appropriate focus is on subsidies conferred on upstream input producers.

---

[7] *United States – Countervailing Measures Concerning Certain Products from the European Communities* (2002) WT/DS212/AB/R.

[8] *United States – Subsidies on Upland Cotton* (AB-2004–5).

D. Export Contingency[9]

With respect to prohibited subsidies that under Article 3 of the SCM Agreement encompass subsidies contingent upon export performance or the use of domestic over imported goods, both types of subsidies have been held to embrace both de jure and de facto contingency. In the case of export subsidies, according to the Appellate Body in *Canada – Aircraft* facts that demonstrate a grant of a subsidy, a "tie to" exports, and actual or anticipated exportation or export earnings, are necessary to demonstrate de facto contingency; it is not sufficient to demonstrate solely that a government granting a subsidy anticipated that exports would result. Annex 1 of the SCM Agreement lists 12 illustrative export subsidies. Export guarantee or insurance programs may constitute a prohibited subsidy under Item J of the Appendix where offered at rates that do not cover the long-term operating costs and losses of the program. The Appellate Body in *U.S. – Cotton 21.5*[10] held that to the extent relevant data are available, an analysis under Item J should involve a quantitative evaluation of the financial performance of a program, taking into account historical data as well as projections regarding the future performance of a program. In *Brazil – Aircraft*,[11] the Appellate Body made it clear that where export credit, insurance, or guarantee programs did not meet these requirements, a country conferring such subsidies would not be excused simply because the withdrawal of such subsidies may entail breaches of contracts with foreign buyers. An important issue that has emerged in the wake of the recent global financial crisis is the potential for currency wars over allegedly undervalued currencies (such as the Chinese yuan), which make exports relatively cheap and imports relatively expensive, leading to massive trade surpluses in the case of China and threatened invocation of

---

9   For an extensive review of the rules and case law of export subsidies, see Andrew J. Green and Michael J. Trebilcock, "The Enduring Problem of World Trade Organization Export Subsidy Rules," in Kyle W. Bagwell, George A. Berman and Petros C. Mavroidis (eds.), *Law and Economics of Contingent Protection in International Trade* (Cambridge University Press, 2010).

10   *United States – Subsidies on Upland Cotton – Recourse to Article 21.5 of the DSU by Brazil* (2008) WT/DS267/AB/RW.

11   *Brazil – Export Financing Programme for Aircraft 21.5* (1990) WT/DS46/AB/R.

countervailing duties by importing countries, especially the U.S., on the grounds that undervalued currencies are an illegal export subsidy. However, it may be difficult to demonstrate that such "subsidies" are contingent on exports but affect all trade – both exports and imports.

E. Adverse Effects

In the case of actionable subsidies, the complaining member must demonstrate adverse effects from such subsidies. In *U.S. – Cotton*, these adverse effects were found to entail price suppression in the world market for Upland Cotton as a result of various U.S. domestic subsidies to cotton producers. In the case of *E.C. – Large Civil Aircraft*, E.C. subsidies to Airbus were found to have adverse effects on Boeing in terms of displacement of imports into the E.C. market, displacement of exports from third country markets, and lost sales more generally.

F. Remedies

With respect to multilateral remedies, Article 4.7 of the SCM Agreement indicates that if a measure is to be found to be a prohibited subsidy, the Panel is to recommend that the subsidy be withdrawn without delay. Where a member fails to withdraw a prohibited subsidy following the Panel's recommendation to this effect, a complaining party may take appropriate countermeasures. In *Brazil – Aircraft*,[12] the arbitrators determined that the scale of the countermeasures may equal the total amount of the subsidies, and in *Canada – Aircraft*[13] indicated that the penalties must be sufficiently large to bring about compliance and to this end added a 20 per cent penalty on top of the value of the subsidies when Canada indicated that it did not propose to withdraw the offending subsidies. In *U.S. – FSC*, the complaining party (the E.U.) was permitted to take countermeasures equal to the full subsidy even though it was not the only

---

[12] *Brazil – Export Financing Programme for Aircraft Recourse to Arbitration by Brazil under Article 22.6 of the DSU* (2000) WT/DS46/AB R.

[13] *Canada – Export Credits and Loan Guarantees for Regional Aircraft – Recourse to Arbitration under Article 22.6 of the DSU* (2003) WT/DS222/AB R.

party harmed. In the case of actionable subsidies, Article 7.9 of the SCM Agreement permits complaining parties only to take counter-measures commensurate with the degree and nature of the adverse effects determined to exist.

V. NORMATIVE RATIONALES FOR DISCIPLINES ON SUBSIDIES

The scholarly literature on normative rationales for disciplines on subsidies does not yield a strong consensus.[14] The most straight-forward justification prohibiting some subsidies relates to their potential to nullify or impair prior tariff concessions. For example, if country A reduces its tariffs on a particular class of imports from 10 per cent to 0 in return for reciprocal commitments by country B, country A could negate the benefit of these concessions by provid-ing subsidies to domestic producers in the amount of 10 per cent of their production costs. This might well yield a claim for nullification and impairment of reasonably expected benefits to country B under Article XXIII of the GATT. In similar vein, it might be argued that if country A has bound its tariff on a particular class of imports to 10 per cent in prior tariff negotiations, then if country B subsidizes exports to country A in an amount equivalent to this tariff, this may arguably undermine the ability of country A to set its tariffs in reciprocal negotiations, thus nullifying or impairing this prerogative under the GATT. However, it will be obvious from the foregoing discussion that the disciplines on subsidies contained in the SCM Agreement range well beyond protecting benefits from prior tariff negotiations.

With respect to the per se prohibition on export subsidies, some commentators argue that these subsidies benefit consumers in importing countries more than any losses suffered by producers in these countries, and should be welcomed by importing countries rather than condemned through either countervailing duty actions or multilateral complaints, while recognizing that third country

---

[14] For a provocative recent review of this literature, see Alan O. Sykes, "The Questionable Case for Subsidies Regulation: A Comparative Perspective," Stanford Law and Economics Olin Working Paper Series No. 380 (2009).

exporters may have a legitimate complaint that their exports are being squeezed out of the importing country's markets by subsidies originating in the first country. Along the same lines, it is argued that export subsidies increase trade, rather than reduce it (as in the case of tariffs) and may assist in mitigating sources of imperfect competition in importing countries. Other commentators argue to the contrary that pure export subsidies have no rationale other than distorting trade and cannot generally be justified on various non-trade related public policy grounds which might justify various forms of domestic subsidies. Moreover, it is argued that export subsidies may lead to subsidy wars (as with agricultural subsidies in various export markets in the 1980s and 1990s), reflecting a Prisoner's Dilemma or race-to-the-bottom, which a highly categoric prohibition agreed to by all member states can preempt.

With respect to actionable subsidies, it is argued that the distinction between specific and general subsidies is arbitrary and often unprincipled and does not recognize legitimate non-trade-related public policy rationales for many specific subsidies; that no effort is made to distinguish between competitively salient subsidies that affect a recipient firm's marginal cost function and hence output from subsidies that benefit it in other ways, for example off-setting plant decommissioning costs or underwriting severance payments, or retraining costs for redundant workers; that no attempt is made to net out the effect of subsidies against other special tax or regulatory burdens that recipient firms may be required to bear; and that in evaluating adverse effects from subsidies, no attempt is made to net out these effects from subsidies or other kinds of benefits to firms from governments in complainant countries.

One approach that has some appeal would be 1) to facilitate sector-specific negotiations among members on subsidy constraints (e.g., agriculture, civil aircraft) to minimize the risk of mutually destructive subsidy wars; 2) to continue the prohibition on export subsidies and import substitution subsidies, defining export subsidies (somewhat arbitrarily) as subsidies applied to the output of firms or an industry where, for example, 80 per cent of output is exported and confine the scope of unilateral countervailing duty remedies to such subsidies; 3) to retain the option of bringing a complaint for nullification and impairment where prior tariff commitments are allegedly being negated by subsidies; and 4) with respect to all other subsidies (specific or otherwise) that can be demonstrated to have adverse effects on other member countries to permit a range of non-trade-related justifications for such subsidies (analogous to those set out in Article 31 of the Tokyo Round Subsidies Code, Article 8 of the SCM Agreement on non-actionable subsidies, and Article XX of the GATT), provided that these are the least trade-restrictive means available for achieving such non-trade-related policy goals (analogous to the necessity test under Article XX), and provided that they meet conditions like those in the chapeau to Article XX, in particular that they are not a disguised restriction on or distortion of trade. The distinction between specific and non-specific subsidies drawn in the SCM Agreement purports to be a descriptive distinction but cannot be reasonably treated as a normative proxy for potential non-trade-related rationales for subsidies that have unavoidable trade spillovers. Only in the event of adverse determinations on these issues would retaliatory sanctions be available. Such a regime would put subsidies and tariff and quota constraints on a similar legal footing.

8. Safeguards and adjustment assistance policies

I. INTRODUCTION

Since the genesis of the GATT in 1947, the multilateral trade regime has provided for unilateral opt-outs from trade liberalization commitments in circumstances involving unforeseen developments causing serious injury to domestic producers in the importing country. Between January 1995 and October 2009, 208 safeguard investigations were reported to the WTO compared to 3427 dumping actions reported to the WTO between 2005 and 2008.[1] While the "safeguards" regime has been much less frequently invoked than the other two major trade remedy regimes (especially antidumping), it has given rise to a number of high profile recent disputes.

Article XIX of the GATT sets out the basic safeguard regime:

> If, as a result of unforeseen developments and of the effect of the obligations incurred by a contracting party under this Agreement, including tariff concessions, any product that is being imported into the territory of that contracting party in such increased quantities and under such conditions as to cause or threaten serious injury to domestic producers in that territory of like or directly competitive products, the contracting party shall be free, in respect of such product, and to the extent and for such time as may be necessary to prevent or remedy such injury, to suspend the obligation in whole or in part or to withdraw or modify the concession.

Article XIX goes on to provide that before any contracting party shall take action pursuant to this provision, it shall give notice to the contracting parties at large and afford those contracting parties

---

[1] Bown, Chad, *Self-enforcing Trade: Developing Countries and WTO Dispute Settlement* (Washington, D.C.: Brookings Institution, 2009), Table 4.3.

having a substantial interest as exporters of the product concerned an opportunity to consult with it in respect of the proposed action. Such consultations may lead to the negotiation of compensatory trade concessions. If compensation cannot be agreed on, affected contracting parties may suspend substantially equivalent concessions or other obligations under the GATT.

Many of the terms and concepts employed in Article XIX are extraordinarily vague, and efforts were made during the Tokyo Round, culminating in the late 1970s, to negotiate a more detailed safeguards code. However, these negotiations foundered over disagreements as to whether safeguards should be permitted on a selective, as opposed to a non-discriminatory basis; whether compensation, in the form of offsetting trade concessions, or in the absence of agreement on compensation, retaliation should be permitted where legitimate safeguard action has been taken; how "serious injury" should be defined; whether there should be political discretion in the imposition of safeguard measures (as opposed to administrative determinations as under antidumping and countervailing duty laws); and the role for multilateral oversight of the invocation of safeguard measures.

At the time of these abortive negotiations and thereafter, circumventions of the requirements of the GATT safeguard regime began to proliferate through the negotiation of bilateral Voluntary Export Restraint agreements or Orderly Marketing Agreements between importing and exporting countries, typically initiated by importing countries with industries experiencing economic distress in the face of intensifying import competition.

During the Uruguay Round, a new multilateral Agreement on Safeguards was finally negotiated. Under Article 4, "serious injury" is defined to mean "a significant overall impairment in the position of a domestic industry". "Threat of serious injury" shall be understood to mean serious injury that is clearly imminent and shall be based on facts and not merely on allegation, conjecture or remote possibility.

Under Article 4(2)(a), in an investigation to determine whether increased imports have caused or are threatening to cause serious injury to a domestic industry, the competent domestic authorities must evaluate all relevant factors of an objective and quantifiable nature having a bearing on the situation of that industry, in particular the rate and amount of the increase in imports of the product concerned in absolute and relative terms, the share of the domestic market taken by increased imports, changes in the levels of sales, production, productivity, capacity utilization, profit and losses, and employment. Under Article 4(2)(b), an affirmative determination must not be made under Article 4(2)(a) unless an investigation demonstrates, on the basis of objective evidence, the existence of a causal link between increased imports of the product concerned and serious injury or threat thereof. When factors other than increased imports are causing injury to the domestic industry at the same time, such injury shall not be attributed to increased imports.

Under Article 2.2, safeguard measures shall be applied to a product being imported irrespective of its source. Under Article 5.2, where a safeguard measure takes the form of a quota, the country adopting the safeguard measure shall allocate the quota to members having a substantial interest in supplying the product shares based upon the proportions of imports supplied by such members during a previous representative period. A country may depart from this requirement of non-discrimination if it can demonstrate to the WTO Committee on Safeguards that 1) imports from certain members have increased disproportionately in relation to the total increase of imports of the product concerned in the representative period; 2) the reasons for the departure from a non-discriminatory allocation of quotas are justified; and 3) the conditions of such departure are equitable to all suppliers of the product concerned. The duration of any such exceptional measures shall not extend beyond four years.

Under Article 7, safeguard measures may not exceed four years in duration, unless the competent authorities of the importing country have determined that the safeguard measure continues to be necessary to prevent or remedy serious injury and that there is evidence that the industry is adjusting, in which case the measure may be renewed provided that it does not exceed eight years duration in total. Under Article 7, safeguard measures shall be progressively liberalized at regular intervals during the period of application. No safeguard measure shall be applied again to the products which have been subject of such measure for a period of time equal to that during which such measure had been previously applied.

Under Article 8, the right of exporting countries to suspend equivalent trade concessions shall not be exercised for the first three years that a safeguard measure is in effect (substantially reducing their ability to insist on compensatory offsetting trade concessions for this period).

Under Article 11, member countries shall not seek, take, or maintain any Voluntary Export Restraints, Orderly Marketing Agreements, or any other similar measures on the export or import side. Such measures must be phased out or brought into conformity with this Agreement within four years after the entry into force of the Agreement.

While this chapter focuses on the GATT safeguard regime under Article XIX of the GATT and the Uruguay Agreement on Safeguards, it is important to note specific safeguard regimes contained in the Uruguay Agreement on Agriculture (Article 5), in the General Agreement on Trade in Services (GATS) (Article X), and in the Agreement on Apparel, Textiles, and Clothing (Article 6), and a specific safeguard regime associated with acceding countries (particularly targeted at China).[2]

Despite these reforms, safeguard actions have led to a significant number of formal trade disputes.[3] A number of these cases have resulted in Panel or Appellate Body decisions.[4] In each of these cases (except *Argentina – Peaches*), WTO Panel decisions have been appealed to the Appellate Body. In not one of the cases did the safeguard measure in question survive challenge. In a withering critique

---

[2] See Mavroidis, Messerlin, and Wauters, *supra* Chapter 6, note 1, Chapter 14.

[3] Leitner and Lester, *supra* Chapter 2, note 3 at 184.

[4] *Korea – Definitive Safeguard Measure on Imports of Certain Dairy Products* (1999) WTO Docs WT/DS98/R and WT/DS98/AB/R [*Korea – Dairy* 1999]; *Argentina – Safeguard Measures on Imports on Footwear* (1999) WTO Docs WT/DS121/R and WT/DS121/AB/R [*Argentina – Footwear*, 1999]; *United States – Safeguard Measures on Imports of Fresh, Chilled or Frozen Lamb Meat from New Zealand and Australia* (2000) WTO Docs WT/DS/177/R and WT/DS178/R and (2001) WTO Docs WT/DS/177/AB/R and WT/DS178/AB/R [*U.S. – Lamb*, 2001]; *United States – Definitive Safeguard Measures on Imports of Wheat Gluten from the European Communities* (2000) WTO Docs WT/DS166/R and WT/DS166/AB/R [*U.S. – Wheat Gluten*, 2000]; *United States – Definitive Safeguard Measures on Imports of Circular Welded Carbon quality Line Pipe from Korea* (2001) WTO Docs WT/DS202/R and (2002) WTO Docs WT/DS202/AB/R [*U.S. – Line Pipe*, 2001]; *Argentina – Definitive Safeguard Measure on Imports of Preserved Peaches* (2003) WTO doc. WT/DS238/R [*Argentina – Peaches*, 2003]; *United States – Definitive Safeguard Measures on Imports of Certain Steel Products* (2003) WTO Docs WT/DS248/R, WT/DS249/R, WT/DS251/R, WT/DS252/R, WT/DS253/R, WT/DS254/R, WT/DS258/R, WT/DS25/R and WT/DS248-259/AB [*U.S. – Steel*, 2003].

of these decisions, Professor Alan Sykes argues that the current safeguard regime, as interpreted by the Appellate Body, has become essentially impossible to comply with, creating strong incentives for member countries to resort again to extra-legal arrangements, such as Voluntary Export Restraint Agreements or Orderly Marketing Agreements, which the Agreement on Safeguards sought to outlaw, and which are in many cases more distorting of trade than formal safeguard measures.[5]

II. SUBSTANTIVE REQUIREMENTS OF THE GATT/WTO SAFEGUARDS REGIME

In Canada, domestic producers petition the Canadian International Trade Tribunal and in the U.S., the International Trade Commission, for determinations that safeguard measures are justified and conse-quential recommendations to the executive arm of government – in Canada, the Minister of Finance, in the U.S., the President of the U.S. – for the negotiation of safeguard measures with affected exporting countries, and in the absence of negotiated agreements, the unilateral imposition of safeguard measures, with the possibility thereafter of affected exporting countries suspending trade conces-sions of equivalent value.

In order for a country validly to invoke the GATT/WTO Safeguard Regime, as set out in Article XIX of the GATT and the Uruguay Round Agreement on Safeguards, certain basic conditions must be met:

A. Unforeseen Developments

Under Article XIX of the GATT, the increase in imports must be a result of "unforeseen developments". This raises the questions of at what point of time must developments have not been foreseen and by whom? As Sykes points out,[6] under U.S. trade law and that

---

5   See Alan O. Sykes, "The Persistent Puzzles of Safeguards: Lessons from the Steel Dispute," (2004) 7:3 *Journal of International Economic Law* 523; Sykes, "The Safeguards Mess: A Critique of Appellate Body Jurisprudence," (2003) 2 *World Trade Review* 261.
6   Sykes, "The Persistent Puzzles of Safeguards", *ibid.*

of many other countries, this requirement had been progressively ignored, and the Uruguay Round Agreement on Safeguards notably fails to mention any such requirement. However, the Appellate Body in *Argentina –Footwear*[7] and *Korea – Dairy*[8] held that Article XIX of the GATT and the Agreement on Safeguards must be read cumulatively, and the Agreement on Safeguards should not be interpreted as abrogating this requirement in Article XIX. It now seems clear from the Appellate Body case law that the relevant point of time for determining whether developments have been unforeseen is when the last tariff concession was made with respect to the class of product in question. An unforeseen development is one that was "unexpected" by trade negotiators at the time when such concessions were negotiated.[9] In a series of cases, both WTO Panels and the Appellate Body have interpreted this requirement relatively strictly and have insisted that only increases in imports attributable to unforeseen developments can be considered in determining whether increasing imports are causing serious injury.

B. Prior Obligations

As noted above, prior obligations have been interpreted to refer to the last point in time at which the importing country seeking to impose a safeguard measure made binding tariff or other commitments related to the product in question.

C. Increased Imports

In *Argentina – Footwear*[10] the Appellate Body held that whether imports are increasing requires consideration of trends over a representative period (often five years), not simply the end points of this period and emphasized that not any increase is sufficient but must have been "recent enough, sudden enough, sharp enough, and significant enough, both quantitatively and qualitatively, to cause or threaten to cause serious injury."

---

7   *Argentina – Footwear* 1999, *supra* note 4.
8   *Korea – Dairy* 1999, *supra* note 4.
9   *Argentina – Footwear* 1999, *supra* note 4.
10 *Argentina – Footwear* 1999, *supra* note 4.

D. Serious Injury

The Appellate Body has held that "serious injury" connotes a significantly higher or more serious level of injury than "material injury" that is the counterpart requirement in antidumping and countervailing duty determinations.[11] Moreover, both WTO Panels and the Appellate Body have insisted that domestic authorities, pursuant to Article 4(2)(a) must, in their determinations, evaluate all relevant factors of an objective and quantifiable nature listed in this provision bearing on the condition of the domestic industry.

E. Causation

While the Appellate Body has held, somewhat confusingly, that increased imports need not be the only cause of serious injury, and other contributing factors may not necessarily preclude such a determination,[12] it has also insisted on a rigorous application of the non-attribution requirement in Article 4(2)(b), pursuant to which when factors other than increased imports are causing injury to the domestic industry at the same time, such injury shall not be attributed to increased imports, and has required domestic authorities to demonstrate that they have rigorously identified all causal factors bearing on a domestic industry's financial distress and carefully assigned relative weights to factors relating to serious injury that are properly attributable to imports and those that are not.

In addition, WTO Panels and the Appellate Body have insisted that where all exports are included in the serious injury determination, but that the safeguard measure itself excludes imports from certain countries (e.g., pursuant to Free Trade Agreements with these countries), the injury determination will be viewed as flawed, in that there must be "parallelism" between the exports included in the injury determination and the exports included in the safeguard measure.

Finally, and more generally, Sykes is highly critical of what he regards as an economically incoherent conception of causation adopted by WTO Panels and the Appellate Body in many of their

---

[11]   *U.S. – Lamb* 2000, *supra* note 4.
[12]   *U.S. – Wheat Gluten* 2000, *supra* note 4.

safeguard decisions by essentially equating correlation with causation. As Sykes points out, increasing imports are often the *result*
of various factors that have caused a shift in either the domestic
demand curve or the domestic supply curve (e.g., an unexpected
increase in the costs of domestic suppliers) and are not the cause
of loss of domestic market share or other measures of the financial
health of the domestic industry. This critique parallels similar critiques of causation determinations in antidumping and countervailing duty determinations. Even with respect to correlation analysis,
Sykes is critical of several WTO Panel and Appellate Body decisions
for accepting, on the one hand, an arbitrary period of trend analysis
by domestic authorities (e.g., five years prior to the safeguard determination), while at the same time insisting that trends in the most
recent months or year or so of this trend analysis be assigned much
more weight than longer-term trends which may be a much more
reliable indication of the need for the domestic industry to undergo
long-term structural adjustment.

Alternatives to correlation analysis reviewed by Sykes include the
hypothetical quota approach, where at the beginning of some representative time period (e.g., the previous five years before the safeguard determination), a hypothetical quota is imposed on imports
and then a determination is made as to whether the domestic industry
would have suffered substantially less serious injury than the injury
that it is in fact incurring with prevailing levels of imports (although
this approach would, in some cases, provide relief to domestic industries that are suffering from some domestically originating factor).
A yet further approach would be to examine over some representative time period shifts in domestic demand curves, domestic supply
curves, and import supply curves, with a view to determining which
of these three potential shifts has in fact been most responsible for
the decline in the financial health of the domestic industry (although
this implies data-intensive and potentially error-prone general equilibrium econometric analysis).

F.   Standard of Review

An overarching question confronting WTO Panels and the Appellate
Body in reviewing determinations by domestic authorities in safeguard actions, as in antidumping and countervailing duty actions,
as well as in many domestic regulatory contexts such as health,

safety, and environmental regulation, is the standard of review that should be applied to these determinations by WTO Panels and the Appellate Body. While Article 11 of the Dispute Settlement Understanding requires Panels to make "an objective assessment of the facts", the Appellate Body seems to have accepted that this does not require Panels to make a *de novo* determination of the facts but rather the review is both a procedural review of the domestic authority's decision-making processes, and the domestic authority's determinations must meet some minimum standard of substantive rationality ("a reasoned and adequate explanation of how the facts support their determination").[13]

III. RATIONALES FOR SAFEGUARD REGIMES

A. Economic Rationales

Some authors argue that safeguard regimes permit domestic industries that have lost their competitiveness vis-à-vis imports a "breathing space" to restructure themselves and become competitive again, or at least contract in an orderly temporal fashion to a competitive core, hence moderating the adjustment costs faced by investors, workers, and dependent communities.

B. Political Rationales

Authors such as Kenneth Dam and Alan Sykes argue that opt-out regimes, such as the safeguard regime, reduce the political risks associated with *ex ante* trade liberalization commitments and hence induce political negotiators to undertake such commitments more willingly, although then the question arises whether the same rationale can also justify antidumping and countervailing duty regimes.

---

[13] *U.S.– Lamb* 2000, *supra* note 4 at 18; see more generally, Andrew T. Guzman, "Determining the Appropriate Standard of Review in WTO Disputes," (2009) 42:1 *Cornell International Law Journal* 45.

C. **Fairness Rationales**

One might argue that the adverse impacts of increasing imports of low-priced products may have distributionally and socially unfair consequences for low-paid, low-skilled, immobile workers, and dependent communities. Again, safeguard regimes may have the potential to mitigate these impacts. However, in this respect, it needs to be noted that many empirical studies have shown that safeguard and related forms of protectionist relief often entail costs for domestic consumers that are several orders of magnitude greater than the value of jobs preserved, at least as measured by wage levels in the industry in question. Moreover, it is not clear why the normative case for intervention to mitigate the impact of shocks from low-priced imports is stronger than domestically originating shocks, such as changes in consumer preferences, technological innovation, exhaustion of natural resources, or various cost shocks. In any event, if this rationale is to be relied on as a justification for safeguard measures, the conception of serious injury embodied in the WTO Agreement on Safeguards would require radical revision to focus not primarily on injury to domestic industries, but injury to domestic workers and dependent communities.

IV. ALTERNATIVES TO SAFEGUARDS

A. **Industrial Subsidies**

In general, industrial subsidies have not been effective in avoiding the ultimate need for adjustment by uncompetitive domestic industries or moderating its severity. Pure output-sustaining subsidies have been the least effective in this respect. Other forms of industrial subsidies have been designed to facilitate the modernization of obsolete capital, but obsolete plants are often the result and not the cause of loss of international competitiveness and if an adequate return could be made on new fixed assets, presumably private capital markets would provide the funds required to make this investment. Less frequently, industrial subsidies have been provided to ease exit costs, where, as in the case of Japan, government plays an active role in managing contraction in demand for domestic industry's output, perhaps through recession cartels, active promotion of mergers or specialization agreements, or compensation for scrapping physical capacity, although such active involvement by government in orchestrating an industry's future shape and size raises questions about both institutional competence and the potential risks for facilitating anti-competitive forms of industry collusion under the guise of industry-wide coordination of efforts at restructuring.

B. Labour Market Adjustment Policies

The normative case for such policies seems much stronger than for industrial subsidies, where workers are often less able to diversify the risks of future shifts in comparative advantage than investors in domestic firms. Most developed countries have introduced some form of unemployment insurance, while a smaller sub-set of such countries have tended to place much more weight on active labour market policies (ALMPs) focused on assistance with job search, relocation, and retraining (safety nets versus trampolines). In general, the latter class of policy seems to have been more effective in mitigating adjustment costs than purely passive forms of unemployment insurance, although the empirical evidence is mixed and in the case of unemployed youths, especially high school dropouts, and older workers, ALMPs seem to have been much less effective than in the case of other classes of workers.

V. REFORMING THE SAFEGUARDS REGIME

Various reforms could be contemplated, from the modest to the ambitious. At the modest end of the scale, there may be much to be said for Sykes' view that the unforeseen development requirement in Article XIX should be removed, and that the causation requirement, at least as interpreted by the Appellate Body, should be substantially relaxed or at least simplified, perhaps through the adoption of something as simple, albeit crude, as the hypothetical quota approach. At the more ambitious end of the reform spectrum, radical reconceptualization of the injury test might be justified, so as to focus on adverse impacts of imports on disadvantaged workers and dependent communities (taking into account other labour market adjustment policies in place).

9. Trade and agriculture

I. INTRODUCTION

Trade in agricultural products has long been one of the most prominent and acrimonious issues on the global trade agenda. Prior to the Uruguay Round, the GATT placed many fewer disciplines on agricultural trade than on any other product sector. Although Article XI of the GATT prohibits quantitative restrictions, it contains a number of exceptions which relate specifically to agricultural trade. In particular, Article XI.2(a) permits export prohibitions or restrictions temporally applied to prevent or relieve critical shortages of foodstuffs or other products essential to the exporting contracting party. Article XI.2(c) permits import restrictions on any agricultural or fisheries product necessary to the enforcement of government measures which operate: i) to restrict the quantities of the like domestic product permitted to be marketed or produced, or ii) to remove a temporary surplus of the like domestic product. In principle, any restrictions applied under Article XI.2(c)(i) shall not be such as will reduce the total of imports relative to the total of domestic production, as compared with the proportion that might reasonably be expected to rule between the two in the absence of restrictions, although this provision has not been rigorously enforced. Article XI.2(c)(i) is particularly important, because it permits countries to restrict imports in order to sustain domestic supply management schemes designed to increase the price of domestic agricultural products.

Apart from Article XI, Article XVI of the GATT provides that contracting parties should seek to avoid the use of subsidies on the export of primary products. Where such subsidies are used, they shall not be applied in a manner which results in that contracting party having more than an equitable share of world export trade in that product, account being taken of the shares of the contracting parties in such trade in the product during a previous representative period. This provision was largely carried over into the Tokyo Round Subsidies Code negotiated at the end of the 1970s. Despite the relative laxity of these provisions, the U.S. government sought and obtained a waiver of Article XI GATT obligations in 1955 with respect to a variety of agricultural products, including sugar, peanuts, and dairy products. In a series of cases in the 1980s, the U.S. challenged before GATT panels various E.U. export subsidies on wheat flour and pasta, and domestic subsidies for E.U. users of oil seeds, but adoption of panel decisions in these cases were vetoed by the losing party.

The instruments of agricultural protection are varied. The European Union's Common Agricultural Policy has traditionally employed a combination of minimum prices for sales within the E.U. protected through variable import levies, guaranteed sales (i.e., government purchase of oversupply), and rebates on export sales below E.U. prices. These policies tend to result in overproduction and displacement of foreign producers in third country markets. U.S. agricultural protection has focused on price support measures coupled with production restrictions, and in recent years certain forms of export subsidies. Canada maintains marketing and production restrictions on poultry, eggs, and dairy products through the use of domestic and import quotas, and arguably confers various forms of subsidies on wheat and grain producers through the operation of state trading enterprises.[1] As well, Japan employs a wide range of instruments including price stabilization, supply management, import quotas, and extremely high tariffs. Agricultural protection imposes costs on consumers through higher food prices, on taxpayers who fund government subsidization programs, and on society through allocative efficiency losses as resources are misdirected toward agricultural production when no comparative advantage exists in this sector. It has been estimated that in 1992 the yearly cost of agricultural protection to non-farm households in Europe, the United States, and Japan (taking into account both higher food prices and higher taxes) averaged $1400 per household per year.[2]

---

[1]　See *Canada – Export Measures Relating to Exports of Wheat and Treatment of Imported Grain* (2004) WT/DS276/AB/R.

[2]　*The Economist*, "Grotesque: A Survey of Agriculture," 12 December 1992, p. 7.

II. THE URUGUAY ROUND AGREEMENT ON AGRICULTURE

During the Uruguay Round, member countries of the GATT committed themselves to beginning an attempt at liberalization of trade
in agricultural products. The negotiations were protracted and
contentious, and raised major divisions between the U.S. and the
E.U. and at various junctures threatened the collapse of the Round.
The opening negotiating position of the U.S. was that all forms of
agricultural support should be eliminated within 10 years, while the
E.U. sought to defend major features of its Common Agricultural
Policy (CAP). Ultimately, a compromise was cobbled together in
the closing months of the Round in 1993. The Agreement addresses
three key sources of distortion in agricultural trade: domestic
support measures (i.e., price supports, payments to farmers, supply
management), export subsidies, and tariffs and non-tariff border
measures. Articles 1(a), 6, and Annex 3 to the Agreement attempt to
quantify domestic support measures in terms of a common metric,
the Aggregate Measure of Support (AMS), and commit members
to 20 per cent reductions in their level of domestic support from a
1986–88 baseline. Articles 8–10 commit members to the reduction of
export subsidies over a six-year period by 21 per cent in terms of the
volume of products that receive subsidies and 36 per cent in terms
of the cash value of such subsidies. Members also commit not to
expand export subsidies beyond the levels reached after achievement
of the six-year goal. It should be noted that this essentially overrides
Article XVI of the GATT, which had theretofore largely permitted
export subsidies on primary products. Article 4 requires members
to convert non-tariff border measures (such as import quotas) into
tariffs, and to reduce overall agricultural tariffs (including non-tariff
measures which have been converted) by at least 36 per cent over
a six-year period, with a minimum 15 per cent reduction in each
product category. Furthermore, new non-tariff measures of any kind
are prohibited. Members also commit to reduce border measures to
an extent that allows foreign producers market access equivalent to 3
per cent of total domestic production, rising to 5 per cent by the end
of the six-year phase-in period.

  The Agreement also includes a system under which certain forms of
subsidies are exempted from the reduction commitments. All forms
of domestic support measures are classified into three categories:

"Yellow Box", "Green Box", and "Blue Box". "Yellow Box" support measures are those which have clear market-distorting effects, such as price supports and other subsidies which encourage overproduction. These measures are subject to reduction commitments. "Green Box" subsidies are defined in Annex 2 to the Agreement, and include measures directed at research, infrastructure, domestic food aid, disaster assistance, training and advisory services. "Green Box" subsidies are deemed to have no effect on trade or production and are exempt from the reduction commitments. "Blue Box" subsidies are listed in Article 6, and involve direct payments to farmers made under "production-limiting programs" and certain developing country subsidies designed to encourage agricultural production. "Blue Box subsidies are not subject to reduction commitments, provided they adhere to certain requirements set out in Article 6.5(a). Article 13 of the Agreement, known as the "peace clause", states that domestic support measures which are exempt from reduction commitments (i.e., "Green Box" measures) are non-actionable for the duration of the peace clause. Furthermore, "due restraint" is to be exercised in initiating countervailing duty investigations into "Blue Box" subsidies. The peace clause expired in January 2004. In *United States – Subsidies on Upland Cotton*,[3] a complaint initiated by Brazil before this expiration date against the U.S. with respect to various U.S. domestic and export subsidies to its cotton producers, users, and exporters, a WTO panel, largely affirmed by the Appellate Body, held that most of these subsidies failed to meet the conditions for immunity stipulated in Article 13 and violated various provisions of the Subsidies and Countervailing Measures (SCM) Agreement. Brazil had also earlier prevailed in a complaint against the E.U. with respect to export subsidies on sugar.[4]

Other important provisions in the Agreement include a safeguard clause, (Article 5) which permits the imposition of additional duties where the volume of imports exceed a given trigger level or where

---

[3]   *United States – Subsidies on Upland Cotton* (2005) WT/DS267/AB/R, discussed in detail by Karen Halverson Cross, "King Cotton, Developing Countries and the Peace Clause," (2006) 9:1 *Journal of International Economic Law* 149.

[4]   *European Community – Export Subsidies on Sugar* (2005) WT/DS265/AB/R, WT/DS266/AB/R, WT/DS283/AB/R [*EC – Export Subsidies on Sugar* 2005].

import prices fall below a trigger price, and Article 15 which provides for special and differential treatment for developing countries. Generally, this treatment entails longer phase-in periods as well as exceptions from the Agreement's disciplines for certain forms of subsidies.

III. THE DOHA ROUND NEGOTIATIONS ON AGRICULTURE

The OECD has estimated that its members' support for agriculture was about U.S. $311 billion in 2000,[5] signifying the modesty of the liberalization efforts reflected in the Uruguay Round Agreement on Agriculture. With a view to launching further liberalization negotiations, Paragraph 13 of the Doha Declaration in 2001 commits member countries to build on the Uruguay Agreement on Agriculture and to negotiate "substantial improvements in market access; reductions of, with a view to phasing out, all forms of export subsidies; and substantial reductions in trade-distorting domestic support." It also agrees to special and differential treatment for developing countries, considering their food security and rural development needs, and to consider the non-trade concerns of member countries. However, these negotiations appear to have reached an impasse. While there appears to be some agreement on phasing out export subsidies (in 1995 the E.U. accounted for 89 per cent of export subsidies),[6] there is much less agreement on reducing domestic forms of support, and severe disagreement over the extremely high tariffs, tariff peaks and tariff escalation which still prevail in this sector and which constitute major barriers to market access. World Bank estimates in 2005 indicated that 90 per cent of the potential gains from further liberalization of agriculture would come from reducing import barriers and 10 per cent from reducing subsidies.[7] The conversion of quantitative restrictions into tariffs mandated by the Uruguay Round Agreement

---

[5] OECD, *Agricultural Policies in OECD Countries: Monitoring and Evaluation 2000* (Paris: OECD, 2000).

[6] See Brett G. Williams, "The WTO Doha Round Draft Text on Agricultural Trade Liberalization: How did We Get into Such a Mess? Should We Walk Away?" (2009) 6: 3 *Farm Policy Journal* at 6.

[7] *Ibid.*

on Agriculture led many countries to substitute tariff rate quotas (TRQs) for former quantitative restrictions and out of quota tariffs sometimes run to several hundred per cent, largely preserving the previous quota system.

Attempts to agree on tariff cutting formulae that would require larger reductions in high tariffs or tariff peaks as well as escalating tariffs on processed agricultural products have foundered. As well, there are sharp disagreements as to the ability of both developed and developing countries to designate some number of agricultural products as "sensitive products" or "special products" respectively, to which tariff reduction commitments would not apply in full or at all and over special safeguard regimes in the agricultural sector. There is also sharp disagreement amongst members as to what special and differential treatment for developing countries should entail. Negotiations have been further compounded by large spikes in food prices that have led some countries to impose taxes or restrictions on some exports to stabilize domestic prices, although exacerbating global price fluctuations. As with the Uruguay Round of Multilateral Negotiations, these issues pertaining to agricultural trade liberalization have proven to be make-or-break issues in the Round.[8]

IV. THE BASIC ECONOMICS OF AGRICULTURAL SUPPLY MANAGEMENT SCHEMES

In understanding impediments to trade liberalization in the agricultural sector, it is important to understand the basic economics of agricultural supply management regimes that set minimum price floors and maximum production quotas for agricultural products

---

[8] For useful surveys of these issues, see Masayoshi Honma, "Agricultural Issues in the Doha Development Agenda Negotiations," in Yasuhei Taniguchi, Alan Yanovich and Jan Bohanes, eds., *The WTO in the 21st Century: Dispute Settlement Negotiations and Regionalism in Asia* (Cambridge University Press, 2007) 328; Williams, *supra* note 6; Tracey D. Epps and Michael J. Trebilcock, "Special and Differential Treatment in Agricultural Trade: Breaking the Impasse," in Chantal Thomas and Joel P. Trachtman, eds., *Developing Countries in the WTO Legal System* (New York: Oxford University Press, 2009) 323.

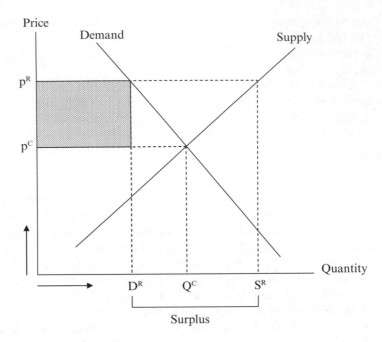

Figure 9.1   Agricultural supply management regime

(e.g., eggs) and that are introduced ostensibly in order to enhance the welfare of small family farmers. The initial impact of the intervention can be graphed as shown in Figure 9.1.

At the competitive price (P^C), quantity Q^C will be demanded and supplied. At the regulated price (P^R), S^R will be supplied but only D^R will be demanded, yielding a surplus of $S^R - D^R$ (the size of which depends on elasticities of demand and supply). The function of maximum production quotas is to ensure that producers only produce D^R so that the market clears. On the demand side, an obvious prediction is that consumers will buy fewer eggs and those that continue to buy eggs will pay more for them, including people of modest means for whom eggs are a staple. On the supply side, assuming production quotas are initially allocated on an historical basis (producers with an established presence in the market), the initial quota recipients will obtain supra-competitive returns, measured by the shaded rectangle, at the expense of consumers who remain in the market. To the extent that some of these initial quota recipients are relatively less efficient egg producers, resources devoted to producing D^R of eggs will be greater than necessary. Quotas might, on that account, be made tradeable to allow more efficient (lower cost) egg producers to produce the eggs demanded at P^R. Prices paid for the quotas will tend to reflect the capitalized value of the future stream of supra-competitive prices (the shaded rectangle). Thus, after paying quota prices, the second generation of egg producers is likely to be making a normal competitive rate of return on its combined investment in egg production resources and quotas. The end result, it would be predicted, would be an allocatively inefficient industry (too few eggs – D^R – are produced), but a productively efficient industry (the low-cost producers service the market after quota transfers), though arguably a distributively perverse outcome in that while small family farmers receive an initial wealth transfer, current egg producers gain nothing from the scheme, and current consumers, including poor consumers, pay more than they need to for eggs. Moreover, the scheme may be politically irreversible, as current egg producers who may have paid substantial sums for quotas to the initial recipients will strenuously resist any termination of the scheme without full compensation (often referred to as "the transitional gains trap" problem).[9]

This example can be readily extrapolated to explain the essential features of the E.U. Common Agricultural Policy, which has turned the E.U. from the world's largest importer of temperate zone agricultural products into the world's second largest exporter. Despite its byzantine complexity, the essential features of the CAP are straightforward. First, as a matter of history, E.U. agricultural producers were guaranteed minimum prices for many classes of agricultural products. However, standing alone, guaranteed price floors raised two problems. First, the floor would be undercut by imports. Hence, the E.U. imposed a variable import levy on imports to prevent price erosion from imports. Second, E.U. consumers would not choose to purchase all the products that would be produced at the guaranteed prices. Hence, the E.U. added to the CAP a commitment to purchase all goods produced at the guaranteed prices. With

---

[9] See Gordon Tullock, "The Transitional Gains Trap," (1975) 6:2 *Bell Journal of Economics* 671.

guaranteed prices and guaranteed purchase commitments, E.U. producers acted rationally and increased supply, creating growing surpluses which the E.U. was forced to stockpile. In order to dispose of these surpluses, the E.U. sold them into third country markets, depressing prices in these markets and squeezing out imports from often more efficient producers in other countries. The difference between export prices and guaranteed domestic prices was financed out of the E.U. budget, accounting for more than half of its total budget. Hence from a domestic scheme designed to increase farmers' incomes within the E.U., the scheme has affected agricultural markets world-wide as a result of export subsidies to surplus production and countervailing subsidies introduced by other countries and are a key and sharply divisive issue in the current Doha Round of multilateral trade negotiations.

V.   RATIONALES FOR SPECIAL PROTECTION OF THE AGRICULTURAL SECTOR

A number of rationales are conventionally advanced for special protection of the agricultural sector in many countries (often encompassed by the concept of "multifunctionality" of agriculture in trade negotiations).

A.   Self-sufficiency/National Security

It is often argued that a nation's survival, in a literal sense, depends upon access to food. In times of shortage, access to food from foreign imports may well dry up or, in any event, reduced dependency on foreigners for food imports may mitigate the risks associated with war or other disruptions of international trade.

B.   Exceptional Price Instability

Some agricultural commodities are subject to much more extreme price fluctuations than those experienced by many other goods that are traded, in significant part because supply is susceptible to unpredictable factors such as weather and hence, as a consequence, farmers' incomes are highly volatile even when they may have a long-term comparative advantage in producing food.

C. Preservation of Rural Lifestyles and the Environment

It is often argued that without special support or protection for small family farmers, food production would increasingly be dominated by large agri-businesses that are heavily mechanized and highly capitalized, and important community values associated with rural lifestyles and family farming would increasingly be undermined. Similarly, it is argued that with the continuing sharp contraction in the number of people engaged in agricultural activities and the continuing exodus of people from rural areas to cities, the rural environment is likely to be increasingly blighted by ugly, polluting industries or replaced by industrial or commercial towns, or simply be depopulated and largely abandoned.

While none of these arguments are bogus, important questions arise in each case as to whether trade protection or other forms of agricultural support are the most appropriate instruments for addressing these concerns. With respect to the self-sufficiency/ national security concerns, few countries can realistically hope to be completely self-sufficient in their food production, and freer international trade enables them to diversify their sources of foreign supply and hence the risk of disruptions in the sources of these supplies. With respect to price instability, much of the agricultural industry in developed countries is now constituted by large commercial producers, and products such as beef, pork, lamb, milk, butter, eggs, and poultry are not subject to the same price fluctuations as crops, fruits and vegetables (although the latter are often an input into the production of the former). Moreover, policy instruments that seek to stabilize farmers' incomes directly, through income-averaging techniques or income insurance, or non-production related subsidies may be more cost-effective instruments than instruments designed to maintain artificially high domestic prices. With respect to concerns over the preservation of rural lifestyles and the environment, a well-conceived regional development plan seems a more finely tuned instrument than agricultural protection to ensure balanced economic activity in rural areas. Much of the potential for reforming agricultural trade comes from the potential for "de-coupling" such policy goals from trade-distorting policy instruments.

D.   Subsistence Agriculture

In many developing countries traditional forms of agriculture are
a critically important source of food sustenance and subsistence
income generation, and may well be threatened by full agricultural
trade liberalization. Traditional farmers in these sectors would face
severe adjustment costs in the event of such liberalization due to
low levels of education and literacy, poorly developed financial
and insurance markets, weak social safety nets, and poor physical
infrastructure. The normative case for providing exceptional forms
of protection or support for these sectors is compelling.[10] Moreover,
tariffs are a major source of government revenue in many developing
countries.

E.   Political Economy Factors

In developed countries, an obvious impediment to trade liberalization in agriculture is the transitional gains trap problem identified
above where trade protection and other forms of support have
been capitalized in land or quota values such that later generations
of farmers who have acquired land or quotas at inflated values
face severe out-of-pocket losses in the event of trade liberalization. Moreover, given the configuration of electoral boundaries in
many countries, despite the continuing exodus of citizens from rural
areas to cities, farmers and rural residents tend to be heavily over-
represented in national legislatures in many countries, conferring
on them a disproportionate political influence. Both these factors
suggest that trade liberalization in developed countries will be a slow
and painful process, and counsel patience and modest expectations
for the agricultural trade liberalization agenda.

VI.   BREAKING THE IMPASSE

Moving forward, high priorities should be the complete prohibition
of export subsidies and a major liberalization of border measures
(tariffs and tariff rate quotas), with few dispensations except for

---

[10]   See Epps and Trebilcock, *supra* note 8.

developing countries with vulnerable traditional subsistence agricultural sectors where special *ex ante* safeguard measures may be warranted. With export subsidies prohibited, and import restrictions substantially liberalized, more latitude should be accorded to domestic subsidies once a much greater proportion of the costs of these are internalized to the countries providing them, precipitating higher internal levels of political accountability for such expenditures.

10. Trade in services

I. INTRODUCTION

The GATT 1947 focused almost exclusively on international trade in goods. However, by the 1980s and 1990s, services accounted for 50 to 60 per cent of domestic GNP in many developed countries, and even higher in the U.S., while international trade in services accounted for only about 20 per cent of total world trade. Hence, as comparative advantage in the production of many manufactured goods shifted to low-wage developing or newly industrializing countries, developed countries became increasingly concerned with enhancing their comparative advantage in many service sectors, such as financial services, telecommunications, transportation, computing, and professional services, by extending the ambit of the GATT to embrace the liberalization of international trade in services. In the Uruguay Round, beginning in 1986, negotiating a multilateral agreement on international trade in services became a priority for many developed countries and resulted in the General Agreement on Trade in Services (GATS) that came into force in 1995.

While the theory of comparative advantage, in principle, seems to apply equally to international trade in services as to international trade in goods, various assumptions that tended to view services markets as largely domestic increasingly came under challenge. First, as a result of technological advances, assumptions that most services required close physical proximity between service providers and consumers became increasingly questionable. Second, while in many countries through most of the post-war period, many important service sectors had been highly regulated, or maintained as state or private monopolies (e.g., in the telecommunications or transportation sectors), regulatory reform movements in many countries during the 1970s and 1980s resulted in the privatization or deregulation of many service sectors, exposing all or large segments of them to domestic competition, and hence then raising further potential for international competition in these sectors. Third, many service sectors were viewed as performing functions integral to the production of goods and as not constituting separate markets in themselves. With the increasing out-sourcing by private enterprises of various inputs into the production of goods during this period, it became increasingly clear that service markets should be properly conceived of as separate from the markets for goods into which they might be inputs.

II. THE GENERAL AGREEMENT ON TRADE IN SERVICES (GATS)

The GATS is in many respects little more than a framework for an ongoing process of multilateral negotiations for liberalizing international trade in services.

A. Scope of the GATS

The Agreement applies to "measures by members affecting trade in services". Measures by members means measures taken by i) central, regional or local governments or authorities; and ii) nongovernmental bodies in the exercise of powers delegated by central, regional or local governments or authorities. Article I of the Agreement defines four modes of supply of international trade in services:

a) from the territory of one member into the territory of another member (cross-border supply);
b) in the territory of one member to the service consumer of any other member (consumption abroad);
c) by a service supplier of one member, through commercial presence in the territory of another member (commercial presence); and
d) by a service supplier of one member, through the presence of natural persons of a member in the territory of any other member (presence of natural persons).

With respect to Mode 4 (presence of natural persons), an Annex to the GATS states that the Agreement does not apply to measures affecting natural persons seeking access to the employment market of a member, nor does it apply to measures regarding citizenship, residence, or employment on a permanent basis.

The Agreement also does not apply to services supplied in the exercise of governmental authority, which means any service which is supplied neither on a commercial basis, nor in competition with one or more service suppliers. This exception has attracted criticism for its limited scope in that many predominantly government-provided services, for example health care, education and water distribution, are provided in competition with private providers and so may fall outside the exception.

B. Most Favoured Nation Treatment

GATS Article II requires that Most Favoured Nation treatment be provided to all trading partners: "Each member shall accord immediately and unconditionally to services and service suppliers of any other member treatment no less favourable than it accords to like services and service suppliers of any other country." A member may maintain a measure inconsistent with Article II provided that such a measure is listed in and meets the conditions of an annex to the Agreement. Under this annex, the Council for Trade in Services shall review all exemptions in force for a period of more than five years to determine whether the conditions which created the need for the exemption still prevail; such exemptions should not exceed a period of ten years. In any event, they shall be subject to negotiation in subsequent trade liberalizing rounds.

C. Domestic Regulation

Article VI of the GATS has proven controversial. Article VI: 4 provides: "With a view to ensuring that measures relating to qualification requirements and procedures, technical standards and licensing requirements do not constitute unnecessary barriers to trade in services, the Council for Trade in Services shall, through appropriate bodies that it may establish, develop any necessary disciplines. Such disciplines shall aim to ensure that such requirements are, *inter alia*: a) based on objective and transparent criteria, such as competence and the ability to supply the service; b) not more burdensome than necessary to ensure the quality of the service; c) in the case of licensing procedures, not in themselves a restriction on the supply of the service.

While these disciplines are still to be developed, critics of the GATS are concerned that they have the potential to constrain greatly the ability of members of the WTO to adopt domestic regulations with respect to services.

D. Specific Commitments

Part III of the GATS covers specific commitments by members. There are two principal types of commitments: Market Access and National Treatment commitments. There is no requirement to make commitments, and commitments which are made may be qualified in any way in which a member chooses, for example by restricting the modes of supply to which the commitment applies. Market access commitments are dealt with in Article XVI, which provides that where market access commitments are undertaken, the measures which a member shall not maintain or adopt either on the basis of a regional sub-division or on the basis of its entire territory unless otherwise specified in its schedule, include limitations on the number of service suppliers; limitations on the total value of service transactions or assets; limitations on the total number of service operations or the total quantity of service outputs; limitations on the total number of natural persons that may be employed in a particular service sector or by a service supplier; measures which restrict or require specific types of legal entity or joint venture through which a service supplier may supply a service; and limitations on the participation of foreign capital in terms of maximum percentage limits on foreign shareholdings or the total value of individual or aggregate foreign investment.

Even though many of these kinds of restrictions may be non-discriminatory, and hence violate neither the MFN nor National Treatment Principles, member countries in the course of negotiations may be prepared to make full or qualified market access commitments designed to enhance market access for foreign service suppliers (in return for reciprocal commitment in these or other sectors).

The National Treatment commitments are dealt with in Article XVII, which provides that members may make either full or qualified National Treatment commitments with respect to the services and service suppliers of any other member in respect of all measures affecting the supply of goods requiring treatment no less favourable than the member accords to its own like services and service suppliers.

Under Article XXI, either Market Access or National Treatment commitments that members have scheduled may be modified or withdrawn at any time after three years have elapsed from the date on which a commitment entered into force, but other members affected by the modification or withdrawal may enter into negotiations with a view to reaching agreement on any necessary compensatory adjustment with respect to other trade measures. If agreement cannot be reached, an affected member may refer the matter to arbitration to determine an appropriate compensatory adjustment. If the modifying member implements its proposed modification or withdrawal and does not comply with the findings of the arbitration, any affected member may modify or withdraw substantially equivalent benefits.

E. Exceptions

Part II of the GATS contains a number of exceptions including Article V relating to economic integration, which is a parallel provision to Article XXIV of the GATT; Article XII that deals with restrictions on trade in services to safeguard the balance of payments; Article XIV, which is a general exception provision that is a close counterpart to Article XX of the GATT but also permits measures of any member "necessary to protect public morals or to maintain public order" (the public order exception may be invoked only when a genuine and sufficiently serious threat is posed to one of the fundamental interests of society), the prevention of deceptive and fraudulent practices or to deal with the effects of a default on services contracts, and the protection of the privacy of individuals in relation to the processing and dissemination of personal data and the protection of confidentiality of individual records and accounts; and Article XIV bis, which provides for national security exceptions and is the counterpart to Article XXI of the GATT.

F. Mutual Recognition Agreements

Under Article VII members who are parties to such agreements may recognize the education or experience obtained, requirements met, or licenses or certifications granted in a particular country.

But parties to such agreements shall afford adequate opportunity for other interested members to negotiate their accession to such an agreement or arrangement or to negotiate comparable agreements with it.

G. Anti-competitive Practices

Article VIII provides that any monopoly supplier of a service in a member's territory shall not act in a manner inconsistent with a member's obligations under the Agreement and specific commitments that it has entered into. Where a member's monopoly supplier competes, either directly or through an affiliated company in the supply of a service outside the scope of its monopoly rights and which are subject to that member's specific commitments, the member shall ensure that such supplier does not abuse its monopoly position to act in a manner inconsistent with such commitments. Under Article IX members recognize that certain business practices of service suppliers may restrain competition and thereby restrict trade in services; each member, shall at the request of any other member, enter into consultations with a view to eliminating such practices.

H. Built-in Negotiations

1. Emergency safeguard measures
Members of the WTO commit themselves to multilateral negotiations on the question of emergency safeguard measures based on the principle of non-discrimination. (Art. X)

2. Government procurement
The Agreement does not apply to regulations or requirements governing the procurement by governmental agencies of services purchased for governmental purposes and not with a view to commercial resale or with a view to use in the supply of services for commercial sale, but members commit themselves to multilateral negotiations on government procurement in services under this Agreement within two years from the date of its entry into force. (Art. XIII)

3. Subsidies
Members recognize that in certain circumstances subsidies may have distortive effects on trade in services and commit themselves to

entering into negotiations with a view to developing the necessary multilateral disciplines to avoid such trade distortive effects and to address the appropriateness of countervailing procedures. (Art. XV)

I. Dispute Settlement

The general dispute settlement provisions of the Dispute Settlement Understanding apply to disputes relating to GATS. The Decision on Certain Dispute Settlement Procedures for the GATS provides that a special roster of panelists is to be established for purposes of settlement of disputes under GATS with expertise in issues relating to the service sectors to which the dispute relates.

J.   The WTO Agreement on Financial Services

Negotiations over financial services commitments were incomplete at the time that GATS came into force, and led to further negotiations that concluded in December 1997 with an Agreement on Financial Services, where many countries made commitments designed to allow the commercial presence of foreign financial service suppliers by eliminating or relaxing limitations on foreign ownership of local financial institutions, limitations on the juridical form of commercial presence, and limitations on the expansion of existing operations. These improvements were made in all of the three major financial service sectors – banking, securities, and insurance.

K.   The WTO Basic Telecommunications Agreement

As with negotiations for the liberalization of international trade in the financial services, negotiations over liberalizing trade in telecommunication services had made limited progress at the time that GATS was concluded, and negotiations were extended and reached a successful conclusion in February 1997, where many countries committed themselves to liberalized trade in international voice services, national long-distance services, local services, data transmission services, leased lines, cellular/mobile telephony services, mobile satellite services, and fixed satellite services, and relaxed restrictions on foreign ownership or control of telecommunication services and facilities. In addition to these commitments, most signatories made commitments to follow the regulatory principles in a Reference

Paper negotiated simultaneously with the other commitments. The Reference Paper requires members to establish appropriate measures to prevent anti-competitive practices by major suppliers, which include cross-subsidization, using information obtained from competitors with anti-competitive results, and not making available to other service suppliers on a timely basis technical information about essential facilities and commercially relevant information which is necessary for them to provide services. Interconnection with a major supplier must be provided, *inter alia*, on a non-discriminatory basis. Other provisions in the Reference Paper relate to transparency and the existence of an independent regulatory regime to resolve disputes *inter alia* over interconnection issues.

III. WTO CASE LAW ON THE GATS

The GATS has attracted relatively little formal dispute settlement activity since it came into force. However, in two relatively early cases – *Canada – Periodicals* (1997)[1] and *E.C. – Bananas* (1997)[2] – the Appellate Body held that in a range of situations where services in question are directly related to trade in goods, both the GATS and the GATT may be applicable and require separate consideration and application.

The leading case on a number of GATS issues to date is *United States – Measures Affecting the Cross-Border Supply of Gambling and Betting Services (Online Gambling).*[3] In this case, Antigua challenged a variety of U.S. federal and state laws and regulatory actions which it claimed amounted to a complete prohibition on the cross-border provision of gambling by Antiguan suppliers. Antigua argued that these prohibitions constituted a violation of U.S. Market Access commitments under Article XVI of the GATS, given that the U.S. had made an unqualified market access commitment with respect to

---

[1] *Canada – Certain Measures Concerning Periodicals* (1997) WT/DS27/AB/R.

[2] *E.C. – Regime for the Importation, Sale, and Distribution of Bananas* (1997) WT/DS27/AB/R.

[3] *United States – Measures Affecting the Cross-Border Supply of Gambling and Betting Services*, 10 November 2004, WT/DS285/R and AB-2005-1, 7 April 2005 [*Online Gambling* 2005].

"other recreational services" which under the UN Central Product Classification Guidelines (CPC) included gambling and betting services. Both the WTO Panel and the Appellate Body held that, indeed, the U.S. was in violation of this commitment, but went on to consider whether the prohibitions were justified under the public morals and public order exception contained in Article XIV(a) of the GATS. The WTO Panel found that U.S. concerns about money laundering, organized crime, protection of minors, and compulsive gambling fell within this exception, taking a reasonably liberal view of the ability of member countries to define the content of public morals and public order based on the beliefs of the nation or community in question as they relate to general or common interests. However, the Panel held that the U.S. prohibition failed to meet the necessity test under Article XIV since it had made no efforts to resolve its concerns through exploring cooperation with the Antiguan authorities as to alternative, less trade-restrictive policies that would as effectively address these concerns.

On appeal, the Appellate Body overruled the Panel on this latter issue, holding that consultations with Antigua could not be considered a reasonably available alternative measure to achieve the U.S.'s public policy goals. Moreover, it held that the U.S. did not bear the burden of demonstrating that every conceivable alternative measure that might be less trade restrictive than the measures in place would be unable to vindicate the U.S.'s public policy goals. Rather, Antigua bore the burden of identifying such a measure, at which point the burden of proof would shift back again to the U.S. to demonstrate that the particular measure identified would not satisfy its public policy goals. However, the Appellate Body went on to hold that, with respect to off-track betting on horse races, the U.S. statute in question, as administered, permitted this with respect to domestic suppliers of gambling services, but not off-shore suppliers, and in this respect violated the chapeau to Article XIV which prohibits the application of the measure in question in such a manner as to constitute arbitrary or unjustified discrimination. Antigua was authorized to impose retaliatory trade measures of $20 million per year, including suspending its TRIPS commitments to the U.S.

IV. CRITIQUES OF THE GATS

The GATS, and the more general agenda for ongoing negotiations to liberalize international trade in services, have attracted intense criticisms from many quarters. For commentators who support the liberalization agenda, the commitments made under the GATS are viewed as extremely modest and disappointing and as amounting to little more than "stand still" commitments, while progress on the built-in negotiating agenda relating to safeguard measures, government procurement, and subsidies, as well as further specific liberalization commitments, have made very little progress. On the other hand, the GATS has attracted intense criticism from anti-globalization commentators, who see in the GATS and in ongoing liberalization negotiations with respect to services an implicit deregulation/privatization agenda which poses serious threats to the domestic political autonomy of member countries, especially with respect to essential services such as water, health care, and education, which have typically been provided in many countries exclusively or primarily by various levels of government and, if open to foreign competition through commitments made under the GATS, would leave governments with very limited future policy flexibility in terms of reversing or modifying policies so implemented. Defenders of the GATS respond by pointing out that member countries assume very few obligations under the GATS unless they choose to schedule Market Access or National Treatment commitments, and even then subject to whatever limitations they choose to impose and that commitments are further subject to modification or withdrawal under Article XXI (subject to negotiation of trade compensation).[4]

V. ALTERNATIVE SERVICE LIBERALIZATION MODALITIES

While the theory of comparative advantage may, in principle, apply equally to international trade in services and international

---

[4] For a critical review of these concerns, see booklet of WTO Secretariat, "GATS – Fact and Fiction" (2001).

trade in goods, the negotiating challenges are much more formidable with respect to barriers to international trade in services than international trade in goods. In the case of goods, historically the challenge has been to negotiate down various border measures, in particular quantitative restrictions and tariffs. In the case of international trade in services, the barriers to international trade are almost never border measures such as quantitative restrictions and tariffs, but internal domestic regulatory policies, and moreover often domestic regulatory policies enacted and administered by sub-national levels of government or delegated agencies of government including professional self-regulatory bodies. These regulatory measures obviously vary dramatically from one service sector to the other, precluding anything analogous to across-the-board tariff cuts and requiring highly transaction-cost-intensive negotiations service sector by service sector. In contemplating alternative negotiating modalities, it is useful to consider the following options.

A.   Non-discrimination Principles (MFN and National Treatment)

Just as these principles have been cornerstones of the GATT, one might argue that non-discrimination, rather than enhanced market access, should be the principal objective of the liberalization of international trade in services. However, in the case of MFN, this has proven problematic, both in the context of negotiations that led to the GATS and subsequent negotiations that led to the WTO Agreement on Financial Services and the WTO Agreement on Basic Telecommunication Services, where the U.S. insisted that it would not make MFN commitments without effective reciprocity from other member countries in order to foreclose the free-riding effect associated with the MFN Principle. With respect to the National Treatment Principle, GATS essentially operates on an opt-in principle, where National Treatment commitments must be affirmatively scheduled under Article XVII. An alternative approach is taken in Chapter 12 of the North American Free Trade Agreement (NAFTA), where the three countries make a general National Treatment commitment with respect to cross-border trade in services, with the right to enter reservations with respect to particular sectors – in effect, an opt-out rather than an opt-in regime. Sectors that are subject to reservations may then be the subject of periodic negotiation or renegotiation. However, as to what exactly the National Treatment Principle requires in particular contexts can be highly problematic. For example, in the case of the self-regulating professions, such as the legal profession, what would constitute conformity with the National Treatment Principle on the part of self-regulating bodies in evaluating and recognizing the credentials of foreign-trained lawyers?

B. Mutual Recognition

Under the Mutual Recognition Principle, which has been extensively applied in the European Union, importing countries agree to recognize home country regulation with respect to service suppliers seeking to provide services in other countries. However, this principle, if unqualified, stands the National Treatment Principle on its head in that it may require importing countries to treat foreign suppliers better than their own suppliers and creates the risk that exporting countries may have incentives to adopt lax regulatory regimes that externalize the negative consequences of ineffective regulation to importing countries, for example with respect to prudential requirements for financial institutions, or licensing requirements for professionals, and may precipitate a race to the bottom. Hence, in practice, the Mutual Recognition Principle is typically accompanied, as it has been in the E.U., with an ambitious agenda for setting minimum harmonized standards for cross-border trade in services. However, these harmonization initiatives crucially depend on an elaborate and sophisticated supra-national institutional apparatus based in Brussels, which finds no ready counterpart in the World Trade Organization or other regional trade agreements.

C. Negotiated Exchanges of Specific Commitments

This is essentially the strategy that had been adopted in the GATS, and finds its counterpart in negotiated product-by-product tariff concessions with respect to international trade in goods in the early rounds of the GATT. However, as has been noted above, these negotiations are likely to be highly transaction-cost-intensive (and not nearly as simple as exchanging tariff concessions) and make significant progress on liberalizing international trade in services a daunting challenge. While in specific sectors such as financial services and telecommunication services, significant progress has been made, the prospects for more general liberalization of international trade in services at the present time do not look strong.

11. Trade and investment

I. INTRODUCTION

Foreign direct investment (FDI) (which is the focus of this chapter) should be distinguished from portfolio investment. FDI typically involves some form of effective control and active management of assets in host countries, while portfolio investment typically involves passive investments in enterprises or government bonds in host countries. Over the last several decades, there has been a dramatic increase in FDI around the world, much of it between developed countries, but increasingly developing countries have been major recipients of FDI, including countries such as China, and in some cases have themselves become exporters of FDI (again, China is a prominent example).[1] More than 40 per cent of world FDI inflows are directed to developing countries. FDI flows to developing countries now exceed foreign aid flows by a factor of about 5 to 1.[2]

In their early post-independence years, many former colonies viewed FDI with skepticism, and in some cases outright hostility, viewing it as holding the potential for creating a new form of economic imperialism (reflected in dependency theories of development that were influential in many developing countries in the 1950s and 1960s). More recently, many developing countries have come to see FDI as having at least the potential for making significant contributions to their economies – as a source of investment in infrastructure, as a source of technology transfers and spillovers, as a source of investment in human capital and skills upgrading, as a source of investment in major natural resource extraction projects, and as a major source of local employment in low-wage, low-skilled

---

[1]   See generally, Americo B. Zampetti and Pierre Sauvé, "International Investment," in Guzman and Sykes (eds.), *Research Handbook in International Economic Law, supra* Chapter 2, note 2.
[2]   UNCTAD, "Assessing the Impact of the Current Financial and Economic Crisis on Global FDI Flows," 19 January 2009.

manufacturing activities. Foreign direct investors, in turn, sometimes see international trade in goods or services and foreign direct investment as complements and in other cases as substitutes. Where host countries have large protected domestic markets, FDI may be the most effective way of accessing these markets behind prevailing tariff walls – particularly the case with host countries with large growing populations and hence significant potential demand for the goods or services that foreign investors can produce. In this case, FDI is a substitute for trade. In other cases, foreign investors are able to expand their opportunities for international trade in goods or services by accessing lower cost inputs (e.g., natural resources or low-cost labour) in host countries and hence gain a comparative advantage in export markets. In this case, FDI and trade are complements.

In principle, the theory of comparative advantage should apply as much to international movements of FDI as to international trade in goods or services – capital is likely to gravitate to where its marginal productivity is greatest. If unqualified, this presumption would suggest the case for an international regime that facilitates the free movement of FDI, and constrains countries from adopting domestic policies designed either to encourage it – for example, through subsidies, tax breaks, or tax incentives – or to discourage it – for example, through regulations pertaining to local sourcing, minimum export requirements, restrictions on exports, trade balancing requirements that restrict the value or volume of imports to the value or volume of exports, technology transfer requirements, and so on. In fact, many countries have adopted a wide range of domestic policies that either encourage or restrict FDI either generally or, more commonly, in particular sectors.

Host countries' restrictions on FDI may be motivated by a range of concerns. First, there are likely to be concerns about foreign investors acquiring domestic firms where the nature of the activities in question raise national security issues – concerns that have been exacerbated by the rapid growth of Sovereign Wealth Funds.[3] Foreign investors who control these assets may have access to sensitive national security technology or information. Second, while there

---

[3]   See Jackie Van Der Meulen and Michael J. Trebilcock, "Canada's Policy Response to Foreign Sovereign Investment: Operationalizing National Security Exceptions," (2009) 47:3 *Canadian Business L.J.* 392.

are few inherent legal constraints on the application of domestic jurisdiction to the activities that foreign investors engage in within a particular country, there may be significant practical constraints in the effective application of domestic laws where the bulk of the firm's assets, many of its senior personnel, and much of the information about its activities and decision-making are located abroad. Third, there may be concerns about attempts by home country governments to enforce their laws in foreign jurisdictions through foreign subsidiaries of home country parent corporations, that is, extra-territorial application of home countries' laws. Fourth, there may also be concerns that foreign subsidiaries will be managed in such a fashion as to reflect home country bias in business decisions, for example purchasing inputs from home country affiliates or using personnel from home country or other affiliates rather than local personnel, perhaps in some cases motivated by a desire to appear to be a "good corporate citizen" in the home country in order to maximize political influence in that jurisdiction. Fifth, there may be concerns that foreign investors will seek to protect their investments in specialized technology and know-how by restricting access to them by domestic firms or individuals in the host country, hence reducing the benefits of technological spillovers and human capital enhancements in the host country.

Foreign direct investors, in turn, are likely to confront their own set of concerns in contemplating investments in a foreign country. These may include political and policy instability (including macroeconomic instability); where investments are sunk, subsequent governments may have incentives to behave opportunistically by unilateral *ex post facto* re-specification of the terms on which the initial investment was made; weak protection of private property rights and ineffective enforcement of contracts; law and order; and corruption in the administration of state functions (including legal functions).

II.   MULTILATERAL REGULATION OF FOREIGN DIRECT INVESTMENT

As has been noted in earlier chapters, historically the GATT was almost exclusively focused on international trade in goods, and not international trade in services or international movement of capital.

However, a GATT panel decision in 1984,[4] in response to a complaint by the U.S. relating to various undertakings obtained from foreign investors pursuant to Canada's Foreign Investment Review Act, held that certain features of domestic foreign investment regulations may fall within the purview of the GATT where these affect international trade in goods. In this case, the U.S. challenged undertakings that required foreign investors to commit to certain local sourcing and minimum export requirements as a condition for approval of their investments in Canada. The Panel held that the local sourcing requirements violated the National Treatment Principle in Article III of the GATT by treating local suppliers of these inputs more favourably than foreign suppliers, although it held that minimum export requirements did not violate any provision in the GATT.

At the beginning of the Uruguay Round in 1986, the U.S. proposed that the multilateral negotiating agenda for this round should include a comprehensive agreement on foreign investment. The Agreement on Trade-Related Investment Measures (TRIMS) that emerged from the Round is, in fact, much more modest than the initial U.S. proposals, and builds on the prior GATT Panel ruling in 1984 by prohibiting domestic regulations that would violate the National Treatment Principle in Article III.4 of the GATT, including local sourcing requirements, trade balancing requirements, and export restrictions. This illustrative list is non-exhaustive. The TRIMS Agreement has attracted very little subsequent formal dispute-settlement activity, in large part because it does little more than reaffirm the application of Article III.4 of the GATT to certain forms of regulation or FDI that may influence imports or exports of goods by foreign direct investors.

Disaffected with this modest outcome from the Uruguay Round, the U.S. and other developed countries sought to shift the venue for multilateral negotiations on a comprehensive investment treaty from the WTO to the OECD, where it was assumed that the predominance of developed countries would yield a readier consensus on liberalizing restrictions on FDI than the WTO where the preponderance of developing country members with more skeptical, or

---

[4]   *Canada: Administration of the Foreign Investment Review Act* (1984) BISD 305/140.

at least cautious, views of the merits of FDI was likely to preclude achievement of a consensus on a more ambitious set of international disciplines. The expectation was that non-OECD members would be able to accede to any resulting treaty and that there would be strong inducements to do so in order to compete effectively for FDI. From 1996 through to 1998 negotiations on a multilateral agreement on investment (MAI) proceeded within the OECD, but negotiations were non-transparent, even clandestine, and the leaking of a draft of the agreement to various NGOs precipitated an international firestorm of criticism of the draft agreement and the process by which it was being negotiated. The principal criticism was that it would confer extensive rights on foreign direct investors but with few, if any, concomitant obligations on their part to host countries or their citizens, for example with respect to technology transfer, health and safety, the environment, labour standards, international human rights, and so on. In the face of these criticisms, the MAI negotiations were formally abandoned in December 1998. Proposals to include negotiations over FDI in the Doha Round of the WTO were also abandoned at the Cancun Ministerial in September 2003 in the face of opposition from developing countries.

III.   BILATERAL INVESTMENT TREATIES

While attempts at negotiating a comprehensive multilateral treaty on FDI appear to have been abandoned, at least for the time being, a notable contrasting phenomenon has been the dramatic prolif-eration since 1990 in the number of bilateral investment treaties (BITS) or international investment agreements (IIAs) that have been negotiated – up from just over 400 in 1990 to more than 2600 today.[5] The primary impetus behind this proliferation of BITS appears to be that in the competition for FDI, many countries, especially develop-ing countries, feel obliged to provide investors with certain legally enforceable protections of their investment, although BITS are not limited to developed–developing country dyads (only about 40 per

---

[5] See Gus Van Harten, *Investment Treaty Arbitration and Public Law* (Oxford University Press, 2007), Chapter 2; Stephen Schill, *The Multilateralization of International Investment Law* (Cambridge University Press, 2009).

cent); about a quarter of all BITS are between pairs of developing countries.[6]

BITS typically include provisions on the scope and definition of FDI; admission of investment; national and most favoured nation treatment; fair and equitable treatment; guarantees and compensation in respect of expropriation and compensation for war and civil disturbances; guarantees of free transfer of funds and repatriation of capital and profits; subrogation on insurance claims; and dispute settlement, both state-to-state and investor-to-state (typically by international arbitration, most often the International Centre for Settlement of Investment Disputes (ICSID) affiliated with the World Bank).

The proliferation of BITS has raised a number of controversies. First, the "fair and equitable" standard of investment protection lacks precision and consistent interpretations or clearly articulated exceptions or qualifications for measures by host countries addressing health, safety, and environmental concerns or financial crises, which has led to criticisms of BITS as unduly constraining host countries' political sovereignty. Second, the expropriation provisions in most BITS also lack clear definition and may be interpreted as extending beyond outright transfer of title to foreign investors' assets or physical dispossession of those assets to various forms of regulatory "takings" that can be viewed as significantly impairing the value of these assets, and this again is criticized for constraining or "chilling" legitimate spheres of regulatory autonomy. Third, given that many countries have signed multiple BITS with various other countries, each of which typically contains a Most Favoured Nation clause, major disputes have arisen as to when foreign investors are able to invoke ("cherry pick") either substantive or procedural provisions in BITS other than the BIT to which their home country is a party which are more favourable to their claims than their own BITS. Fourth, the National Treatment Principle, which is contained in most BITS, also gives rise to ambiguity as to when foreign investors have been treated less favourably than domestic investors in "like circumstances". Fifth, the international arbitral dispute resolution system has been criticized as lacking transparency,

---

[6] UNCTAD, "Recent Developments in International Investment Agreements," IIA Monitor No. 3 (2009).

lacking consistency, lacking scope for effective third-party (amicus) interventions, and in general being biased towards the interests of foreign investors.[7] Finally, it is argued that BITS largely remove foreign investors as a political constituency for domestic legal reform in host countries by providing them with privileged supra-national legal protections.[8]

A new generation of BITS attempts to strike a finer balance between the interests of investors and the interests of host countries by adding interpretive provisions, general exceptions clauses, and new preambular language as to the purpose of the agreements,[9] but how arbitrators are likely to interpret such provisions and whether they are effectively justiciable in a consistent and credible manner remains to be tested by experience. As to whether BITS actually increase FDI flows to host countries that are signatories to them has yielded a rather mixed body of empirical evidence.[10] Perhaps the best reading of this evidence is that BITS have a modestly positive impact on attracting FDI – albeit a declining marginal impact as more BITS are signed – and are a weak substitute for well-functioning domestic legal institutions,[11] in part because arbitral awards still need to be enforced in host countries' domestic courts, and in part because purely private disputes may still need to be resolved in these courts unless the parties have contracted out of the jurisdiction through

---

[7] For a review of some of these critiques, see Graham Mayeda, "Investing in Development: The Role of Democracy and Accountability in International Investment Law," (2009) 46:4 *Alberta Law Review* 1009.

[8] Tom Ginsburg, "International Substitutes for Domestic Institutions: Bilateral Investment Treaties and Governance," (2005) 25:1 *International Review of Law and Economics* 107.

[9] See Suzanne A. Spears, "The Quest for Policy Space in a New Generation of International Investment Agreements," *Journal of International Economic Law* (forthcoming).

[10] See Amnon Lehavi and Amir N. Licht, "BITS and Pieces of Property," 36 *Yale Journal of International Law* (forthcoming 2011) at 11–13. For a recent study finding more positive effects of BITS on FDI, see Matthias Busse, Jens Koniger and Peter Nunnekamp, "FDI Promotion through Bilateral Investment Treaties: More than a Bit?", (2010) 146 *Review of World Economy* 147.

[11] See Susan Rose-Ackerman and Jennifer Tobin, "When BITS Have Some Bite: The Political-Economic Environment of Bilateral Investment Treaties," Yale Law School, 25 April 2007.

(increasingly common) choice of law and choice of forum clauses.[12]

Chapter 11 of NAFTA, while involving three parties, exemplifies many of the issues and controversies that have arisen with respect to BITS and has been a prominent lightning rod for critics of NAFTA. When Chapter 11 was initially negotiated, it was thought likely to apply in practice mostly to Mexican laws and regulations pertaining to FDI, given a long and somewhat tangled history in Mexico of cycles of nationalization and liberalization of FDI. However, Chapter 11 has provoked a number of formal complaints (in excess of 30 to date), including a number against measures adopted in Canada and the U.S.

Chapter 11 of NAFTA contains a National Treatment provision in Article 1102 (subject to reservations that the three parties have entered in schedules to NAFTA) and a Most Favoured Nation Treatment provision (Article 1103). Article 1105 (Minimum Standard of Treatment) requires that each party shall accord to investments of investors of another party treatment in accordance with international law, including fair and equitable treatment and full protection and security. Article 1106 (Performance Requirements) prohibits a long list of performance requirements, including those contained in the TRIMS Agreement but extending to other performance requirements such as technology transfer requirements. Article 1110 (Expropriation and Compensation) provides that no party may directly or indirectly nationalize or expropriate an investment of an investor of another party in its territory or take a measure tantamount to nationalization or expropriation of such an investment except a) for a public purpose; b) on a nondiscriminatory basis; c) in accordance with due process of law and Article 1105; and d) on payment of compensation.

Chapter 11 then sets out a procedural regime for the resolution of disputes which permit private investors to file complaints with international arbitral panels, primarily the International Centre for Settlement of Investment Disputes (ICSID). Awards issued by such arbitral panels providing for monetary compensation for foreign investors who have been able to satisfy an arbitral panel that the host country's measures in question violate one of the substantive

---

[12]   See Jans Damman and Henry Hansmann, "Globalizing Commercial Litigation," (2008) 94 *Cornell L. Rev.* 1.

provisions of Chapter 11 are enforceable in the domestic courts of host countries.

The arbitral case law that has emerged under Chapter 11 has raised major uncertainties as to the interpretation and application of key substantive provisions in Chapter 11, especially the International Minimum Standard of Treatment requirement in Article 1105 and the Expropriation provisions in Article 1110, which different arbitral panels have interpreted both expansively and narrowly but without a system of appellate review or precedent to resolve inconsistencies. Critics of Chapter 11 argue that its provisions and the investor-driven complaints dispute-settlement process have undesirably constrained the domestic political autonomy of member countries and imposed a regulatory chill on legitimate environmental and health and safety measures that host countries have sought or might seek to adopt.[13] Moreover, the expropriation provisions of Chapter 11 risk standing the National Treatment Principle on its head by requiring compensation of foreign investors in circumstances where similarly situated domestic investors may lack any such entitlement.[14]

Other commentators take a more benign view of the operation of Chapter 11, and regard the few decisions that have led to liability as properly sanctioning protectionist or abusive behavior by host country governments.[15] While some of the procedural shortcomings of the dispute settlement process under Chapter 11 have recently been mitigated by member countries in an Interpretive Statement and by reforms by arbitral panels themselves in authorizing the release of the written pleadings of the parties at the time they are filed with an arbitral panel, authorizing *amicus curiae* briefs, and making the oral hearings open to the public, concerns remain about the extent of the substantive constraints on host countries' jurisdiction

---

[13] See Chris Tollefson, "NAFTA's Chapter 11: The Case for Reform," in John Kirton and Peter Hajnal (eds.), *Sustainability, Civil Society, and International Governance* (Aldershot: Ashgate Publishing Limited, 2006), Chapter 10.

[14] See David Schneiderman, "NAFTA's Takings Rule: American Constitutionalism comes to Canada," (1996) 46 *U. of Toronto L.J.* 499; Michael Trebilcock, "Trade Liberalization, Regulatory Diversity, and Political Sovereignty," *ibid* at 224, 225.

[15] See Julie Solway, "NAFTA's Chapter 11: Investor Protection, Integration, and the Public Interest," *ibid*, Chapter 9.

to regulate FDI, particularly given the absence of any provision in Chapter 11 analogous to Article XX of the GATT.

IV. CONCLUSION

The proliferation of BITS stands in stark contrast to successive failures to negotiate a multilateral agreement on investment. However, BITS entail a risk of collective action problems and a race to the bottom among host countries (especially developing countries). This argues for a further attempt at negotiating a multilateral agreement (where coalition bargaining is possible), probably under the aegis of the WTO, building on the new generation of BITS that attempt to strike a better balance between the interests of foreign investors and host countries.

12. Trade-related intellectual property rights

I. INTRODUCTION

Prior to the launch of the Uruguay Round of multilateral trade negotiations in 1986, there were growing concerns in the U.S. and other developed countries over loss of export markets in various developing and newly industrializing countries due to weak protection of intellectual property rights. Some of these concerns related to counterfeit goods and the misappropriation of trademarks (e.g., fake Rolex watches or Pierre Cardin garments). Other concerns related to unauthorized reproduction of sound recordings and videos and breach of copyright held in these recordings or videos by the original performers or their publishers. Further concerns related to substantively lower levels of patent protection and less effective procedural protection of patent rights in many countries, leading to a proliferation of imitation products, including generic pharmaceuticals. For developed countries, which were losing their comparative advantage in low-skilled, "smokestack" manufacturing industries to developing and newly industrializing countries, it became an important priority to seek better protection of their comparative advantage in scientific and technological innovation through stronger protection of intellectual property rights.

As to justifications for extending western-style protection of intellectual property rights to developing newly industrializing countries, proponents relied in part on deontological natural rights (Lockean) theories of labour whereby all individuals can claim a proprietary right to all the fruits of their labour, and hence argued that appropriation by others of the fruits of the labour of innovators was tantamount to "stealing from the mind",[1] although such theories would

---

[1] See Peter Drahos and John Braithwaite, *Information Feudalism* (New York: New Press, 2003), Chapter 4.

seem to imply an infinite duration to intellectual property rights, which manifestly has never been the case. Proponents also in part relied on consequentialist or welfare theories, whereby attenuated returns to innovation as a result of free-riding on the innovations of others would reduce incentives to innovation, reducing long-run social welfare in both developed and developing countries.

On the other side of the debate, it was argued that the additional rents that intellectual property holders could realize in many developing countries were so modest that it was difficult to make the case that the loss of these rents would have a significant impact on incentives to innovate. Moreover, for many developing countries, particularly those at early stages of economic development, their comparative advantage would often lie in imitation rather than innovation, and global welfare requires an appropriate balance to be struck between technological or scientific innovation, on the one hand, and technical and scientific diffusion or dissemination, on the other.

II. THE PRE-URUGUAY ROUND INTERNATIONAL LEGAL FRAMEWORK

A. The GATT

The GATT was almost entirely silent on the relationship between international trade and intellectual property rights, except for Article XX(d) which exempted measures necessary to secure compliance with laws or regulations, including the protection of patents, trademarks, and copyrights, subject to the conditions in the chapeau to Article XX. A GATT panel decision in 1989[2] held that Article XX(d) did not justify the deployment of extraordinary remedies against potentially infringing imports of goods beyond those available against domestic infringers; such remedies were held to violate the conditions in the chapeau to Article XX relating to arbitrary or unjustifiable discrimination.

---

2   *United States – Section 337 of the Tariff Act of 1930* L 6439 (1989).

B.   The Paris Convention (1883)

This Convention, which deals with patents and trademarks, contains a National Treatment Principle, but not an MFN Principle, and sets no minimum level of protection for patents. In the case of trademarks, signatories are obligated to accept trademarks once properly registered in the country of origin.

C.   The Berne Convention (1885)

This Convention deals principally with copyrights, and contains a National Treatment and MFN Principle. It prescribes a minimum length of protection for copyrights – the author's life plus 50 years – with some limited exceptions. Both the Paris Convention and the Berne Convention were administered from 1967 onwards by a United Nations agency, the World Intellectual Property Organization (WIPO).

D.   U.S. Unilateralism

Under Section 337 of the US Tariff Act of 1930 as amended, products imported into the U.S. that have been produced in such a way as to violate intellectual property rights that U.S. individuals or firms hold may be subject to orders requiring the complete exclusion of the product from the U.S. unless the U.S. holder of intellectual property rights and the foreign producer enter into a voluntary settlement (usually a licensing agreement). In addition, where a developing country insists on weak intellectual property protection, tariff concessions extended to it under the Generalized System of Preferences (GSP) can be withdrawn. Finally, under the so-called special 301 provision of the Omnibus Trade and Competitiveness Act of 1977, trade sanctions may be taken against countries engaging in "unfair trade practices", which may include failure to respect or enforce U.S. intellectual property rights in foreign markets.

III. THE URUGUAY ROUND TRIPS AGREEMENT

The WTO TRIPS Agreement was the result of extensive lobbying by high technology firms in the U.S. and other developed countries,[3] and essentially requires all members of the WTO to adopt domestic intellectual property laws that conform to the minimum standards set out in the TRIPS Agreement, which in turn, for the most part, reflect western standards of intellectual property protection.

A. General

The TRIPS Agreement contains a National Treatment Principle (Article 3) and an MFN Principle (Article 4). With respect to the doctrine of exhaustion, Article 6 provides that nothing in this agreement shall be used to address the issue of the exhaustion of intellectual property rights, leaving open divergences between countries that in some cases had adopted a doctrine of national exhaustion and others that had adopted a doctrine of international exhaustion. Under a doctrine of national exhaustion, once an intellectual property holder sells goods in a domestic market, it relinquishes all rights with respect to the goods in subsequent transactions within that market, but not in other markets where the intellectual property holder has enforceable intellectual property rights. Under the doctrine of international exhaustion, the first sale by an intellectual property rights holder in any market extinguishes its rights in all markets, leaving open the possibility of parallel importation of goods from lower-priced markets into higher-priced markets. Article 7 of the Agreement provides that the protection and enforcement of intellectual property rights should contribute to the promotion of technological innovation and to the transfer and dissemination of technology, to the mutual advantage of producers and users of technological knowledge and in a manner conducive to social and economic welfare, and to a balance of rights and obligations. Article 8 provides that members may, in formulating or amending their laws and regulations, adopt measures necessary to protect public health and nutrition, and to promote the public

---

[3]   See Drahos and Braithwaite, *supra* note 1.

interest in sectors of vital importance to their socio-economic and technological development, provided that such measures are consistent with the provisions of the Agreement.

B. Copyright and Related Rights

The basic obligations of the Berne Convention are incorporated into TRIPS. Computer programs and databases are included as literary works (Article 10). The minimum term of protection for copyrighted works is 50 years from the initial date of authorized publication or 50 years from the making of the work.

C. Trademarks

The Agreement requires that all signs with sufficient distinctiveness be accepted for registration by all members (Article 15). Registration may be cancelled only after an uninterrupted period of at least three years of non-use, unless there are valid reasons for non-use based on the existence of obstacles to such use (Article 19). Initial registration and each renewal of registration of a trademark shall be for a term of no less than 7 years (Article 18).

D. Geographical Indications

Members shall provide the legal means for interested parties to prevent the use of any means in the designation or presentation of a good that indicates or suggests that the good in question originates in a geographical area other than the true place of origin in a manner which misleads the public as to the geographical origin of the good (Article 22). Additional protection is required for geographical indications for wines and spirits (Article 23 and Article 24).

E. Industrial Designs

Members are required to provide for the protection of independently created industrial designs that are new or original. The duration of protection available shall amount to at least 10 years (Articles 25 and 26).

F. Patents

Patents shall be available for any invention, whether products or processes, in all fields of technology, provided that they are new, involve an inventive step and are capable of industrial application. Patents shall be available and patent rights enjoyable without discrimination as to the place of invention, the field of technology and whether the products are imported or locally produced (Article 27). Members may exclude from patentability inventions, the prevention within their territory of the commercial exploitation of which is necessary to protect *ordre public* or morality, including to protect human, animal or plant life or health or to avoid serious prejudice to the environment. Members may also exclude from patentability diagnostic, therapeutic and surgical methods for the treatment of humans, and plants and animals other than micro-organisms. However, members must provide for the protection of plant varieties either by patents or by an effective *sui generis* system.

A patent shall confer on its owner exclusive rights to prevent third parties not having the owner's consent from the acts of making, using, offering for sale, or selling a product in which the owner holds a patent (Article 28).

Members may provide limited exceptions to the exclusive rights conferred by a patent, provided that such exceptions do not unreasonably conflict with the normal exploitation of the patent and do not unreasonably prejudice the legitimate interests of the patent owner, taking account of the legitimate interests of third parties (Article 30).

Under Article 31 compulsory licensing is permitted, subject to various conditions, including: i) the proposed user has made efforts to obtain authorization from the right holder on reasonable terms and conditions and that such efforts have not been successful within a reasonable period of time (this requirement may be waived by a member in the case of a national emergency or other circumstances of extreme urgency or in cases of public non-commercial use); ii) such use shall be non-exclusive; iii) such use shall be authorized predominantly for the supply of the domestic market of the member authorizing such use; iv) the right-holder shall be paid adequate remuneration in the circumstances of each case, taking into account the economic value of the authorization.

The term of protection for patents shall not end before the

expiration of a period of 20 years counted from the filing date (Article 33).

Members are required to protect undisclosed information, including information provided to members as a condition of approving the marketing of a pharmaceutical or agricultural chemical product (Article 39).

Nothing in the Agreement shall prevent members from adopting appropriate measures to prevent anticompetitive practices with respect to intellectual property licenses, including exclusive grant-back conditions, conditions preventing challenges to validity, and coercive package licensing (Article 40).

G. Remedies

Every member is committed to ensuring that enforcement procedures with respect to the protection of intellectual property rights are in place that are not unnecessarily complicated, costly or protracted. Members must provide a right of judicial review of administrative decisions. Judicial authorities must have the power to award damages and injunctions and provide interim relief to intellectual property right holders against infringements (Articles 41 to 50). Members are also required to adopt procedures to enable an intellectual property rights holder to lodge an application with competent authorities for the suspension by the customs authorities of the release of infringing goods into free circulation of such goods (Articles 51 to 60). Members shall provide for criminal procedures and penalties in cases of wilful trademark counterfeiting or copyright piracy on a commercial scale (Article 61).

H. Dispute Settlement

The general dispute settlement provisions of the GATT applies to disputes under the TRIPS Agreement, except that the non-violation nullification and impairment provisions of Article XXIII of the GATT did not apply to disputes under the TRIPS Agreement for a period of five years from its entry into force.

I. Transitional Arrangements

Various transitional arrangements are provided for developing countries in terms of extended periods for ensuring compliance of the domestic intellectual property laws with the TRIPS Agreement, but these have all now expired (Article 65), except for certain limited exceptions for least-developed countries with respect to pharmaceutical patent protection, which were extended to 2016 by the Doha Declaration on Public Health, November 2001.

IV. THE ESSENTIAL MEDICINES DEBATE

The TRIPS Agreement, particularly as it applies to access to essential medicines, has been a lightning rod for vehement criticism by anti-globalists and civil society organizations around the world, who allege that developed country members of the WTO in effect have blood on their hands as a result of compelling all WTO members, including poor developing countries, to adopt domestic intellectual property regimes that conform to the minimum (western) standards prescribed by the TRIPS Agreement.[4] The criticisms focus on the fact that prices charged by proprietary pharmaceutical companies in developing countries for essential medicines, like HIV/AIDS antiretrovirals, deny access by most poor citizens of these countries to these lifesaving drugs and prevent, except under stringent conditions, access to much cheaper generics. Moreover, it is argued that 90 per cent of global resources devoted to pharmaceutical research relates to 10 per cent of the world's disease burden, or conversely only 10 per cent of global pharmaceutical research is devoted to 90 per cent of the world's disease burden that is borne mostly by citizens in developing countries.

Critics of TRIPs are also critical of one of the leading WTO dispute-settlement decisions on the TRIPS Agreement: *EU – Canada-Patent Protection of Pharmaceuticals* (2000),[5] where under the Canadian Patent Act, exceptions from 20-year protection of patents were provided with respect to steps necessary to ensure regulatory

---

4   See Drahos and Braithwaite, *supra* note 1.
5   *EU – Canada-Patent Protection of Pharmaceuticals* (2000) WT/DS114/R.

approval of derivative (generic) products before the expiration of the patent on these products and with respect to stockpiling of derivative products for six months prior to the expiration of a patent on these products. A WTO Panel held that the regulatory review exception could be justified under Article 30 of TRIPS (because otherwise the interaction of regulatory review requirements and patent protection could lead to substantial de facto extension of patent terms), but not the stockpiling exception (because all patent protection precludes manufacture of derivative products until after patent expiration).

On the other side of the debate, it is argued that historically weak intellectual property protection in developing countries has provided few incentives for proprietary pharmaceutical industry to invest R & D resources in developing cures for tropical and related diseases that particularly afflict citizens of developing countries, and that the TRIPS Agreement, in principle, resolves a collective action problem among developing countries by committing them all to observe minimum standards of intellectual property protection. Moreover, it is argued that adoption of a doctrine of international exhaustion is likely to undermine efforts by proprietary pharmaceutical companies to practice geographic price discrimination (i.e. charging more to citizens with less elastic demand in richer countries and less to citizens with more elastic demand in poorer countries), in that parallel importation will undermine such efforts.[6]

While the compulsory licensing provisions in Article 31 of the TRIPS provide the potential for alleviating some of the concerns about access to essential medicines, key provisions in Article 31 lack clear definition. For example, prior to issuing a compulsory license efforts must be made within a "reasonable period of time" to obtain authorization from the intellectual property holder on "reasonable commercial terms" (although this is not necessary for a "national emergency" or circumstances of "extreme urgency"), but none of these terms are defined, nor is the requirement that there be payment of "adequate remuneration" where a compulsory license is issued. Moreover, compulsory licenses can only be issued predominantly for the supply of the licensee's domestic market, which in the case of pharmaceuticals is likely to preclude poor developing countries

---

[6] See Alan O. Sykes, "TRIPS, Pharmaceuticals, Developing Countries and the Doha Solution," (2002) 3:1 *Chicago Journal of International Law* 47.

that lack a generic drug manufacturing industry of their own from taking advantage of the compulsory licensing provisions of Article 31.

Criticisms of the TRIPS Agreement as they relate to access to essential medicines led to the Declaration on the TRIPS Agreement and Public Health at the Doha Ministerial Conference launching the new Doha Round of multilateral trade negotiations in November 2001. In this Declaration members reaffirm the right of WTO members to use, to the full, the provisions in the TRIPS Agreement which provide flexibility in protecting public health and promoting access to medicines for all. In particular, each member has the right to determine what constitutes a national emergency or other circumstances of extreme urgency; each member is free to establish its own regime for exhaustion of intellectual property rights without challenge; and the Council for TRIPS was directed to find an expeditious solution to the problem that WTO members with insufficient or no manufacturing capacities in the pharmaceutical sector could face difficulties in making effective use of compulsory licensing under Article 31 of the TRIPS Agreement.

Further to this direction, a Decision of the WTO General Council of 30 August 2003 adopted a detailed set of provisions relating to compulsory licensing of pharmaceuticals where in the case of WTO members with insufficient or no manufacturing capacities in the pharmaceutical sector, compulsory licenses could be issued to generic drug manufacturers in exporting countries and complementary compulsory licenses also be issued by importing countries able to demonstrate the lack of domestic manufacturing capacity. In order to prevent "leakage" of generic pharmaceuticals provided under this regime to other countries, the Decision of the General Council requires that products issued under compulsory licenses pursuant to these provisions should distinguish such products through special packaging and/or special colouring or shaping of the products themselves.

While this Decision of the General Council was initially in the nature of a waiver of inconsistent provisions in the TRIPS Agreement, it is contemplated that it will eventually become a formal amendment to the TRIPS Agreement.

Pursuant to these provisions, Canada in 2004 amended its Patent Act and Food and Drugs Act to permit the issuance of compulsory licenses under the conditions set out in the Decision of the WTO

General Council.[7] Both the Decision of the WTO General Council and the subsequent Canadian legislation have been widely criticized as being much too cumbersome to comply with, in that compulsory licenses in both exporting and importing countries must be issued for every shipment of the drugs in question, and in fact only one compulsory license has been issued to date under the Canadian legislation. Critics argue that an omnibus compulsory licensing regime would be more effective.

Two issues relating to the essential medicines debate warrant concluding comments. First, it is far from clear why proprietary pharmaceutical drug companies, even under the original TRIPS Agreement provisions, would not have found it rational (profit-maximizing) to have engaged in extreme forms of geographic price discrimination, pricing drugs down to close to marginal costs in poor developing countries and recovering their fixed investments in R & D in much richer developed country markets, provided they could be assured that drugs would not "leak" back from the former markets to the latter, thus undercutting their ability to recover their R & D costs in developed country markets. Part of the explanation for this puzzle may be that such extreme forms of geographic price discrimination would reveal to consumers in developed countries how low the marginal costs of production for propriety pharmaceuticals are, perhaps leading to pressures for price regulation in developed countries, although this assumes that consumers in developed countries could not be persuaded that somebody needs to bear the fixed costs of R and D.

Second, while this form of extreme geographic price discrimination has the potential for mitigating the access to essential medicines problems with respect to existing pharmaceuticals in wide use in both the developed and developing world (facilitated by the now more credible threat of compulsory licensing), it is not nearly as clear that the intellectual property regime, even as amended by the Decision of the WTO General Council in August 2003, will ensure that there are adequate investments in pharmaceutical innovations for diseases that are primarily prevalent in developing countries, where there may simply be a lack of effective demand for these products, given poverty level incomes on the part of many citizens and

---

[7] Bill C-9, 14 May 2004.

limited resources on the part of their governments (and no demand in rich countries from which to finance R & D costs). In order to address this problem, one might need to look for solutions outside the intellectual property domain, such as the Global Fund created by the former Secretary General of the United Nations, Kofi Annan or investments by private foundations (such as the Gates Foundation), with a view to entering into R & D contracts with research institutions directed to finding cures for such diseases. In short, public or private foundation subsidies to investments in R & D with respect to tropical and related diseases that particularly afflict citizens in developing countries, are likely to be required if substantial progress is to be made in addressing this problem, although effective design of the qualifications for, and incentive properties of, these subsidy arrangements presents their own set of challenges.

13. Trade policy and domestic health and safety regulation

I. INTRODUCTION

With the progressive liberalization of border barriers to trade over the post-war period, internal or "beyond the border" regulatory divergences from one country to another, including domestic regulation of health and safety standards, have become an increasing source of tension in international trading relations. Exporting countries often complain that these regulations constitute a non-tariff barrier to trade, and even where they are not intended as a disguised form of protectionism, impose disproportionate burdens on small exporting countries, particularly developing countries, in facing multiple compliance costs in many of their export markets. Importing countries, in turn, complain of lax standards in exporting countries that create health and safety risks for their citizens,[1] as well as constituting a form of unfair trade to the extent that firms in exporting countries face lower compliance costs than competing firms in importing countries.

Free traders often propose international constraints on the use of domestic regulations as barriers to trade, while consumer and citizens groups favour constraints on the use of international trade agreements as barriers to regulation. These divergences in perspective have led to divisions between business interests and civil society groups, on the one hand, and between developed and developing countries on the other. Those favouring international constraints on domestic health and safety regulation to address concerns of regulatory discrimination or disguised protectionism often assign pre-eminence to compliance with international standards or scientific

---

[1] See Cary Coglianese, Adam Finkel and David Zaring (eds.), *Import Safety: Regulatory Governance in the Global Economy* (University of Pennsylvania Press, 2009).

justifications, arguing that regulatory protectionism typically entails higher welfare losses than other forms of protectionism (such as tariffs or subsidies).[2] Those favouring fewer constraints on domestic political autonomy in regulating health and safety rules facing a country's citizens emphasize the importance of democratic accountability and responsiveness to public sentiments and concerns of citizens (whether based on science or not),[3] recognizing that public attitudes to risk often do not reflect the tenets of scientific or economic rationality (as the growing body of literature on behavioural law and economics demonstrates).[4]

II. THE GATT FRAMEWORK

A. The Evolution of the GATT/WTO[5]

The original GATT did not contain separate provisions constraining the regulation of domestic environmental health and safety standards. However, bans on imports might violate Article XI, and discriminatory treatment of imports from different foreign countries might violate Article I (MFN), and discriminatory regulation of imports generally relative to domestic like products might violate Article III.4 (National Treatment). In such an event, the regulating country might seek to justify its regulations under Articles XX(b) or XX(g), which provides exceptions from the disciplines of the GATT for trade measures necessary to protect human, animal, or plant life or health, or relating to the conservation of natural resources. However, during the Tokyo Round, the Agreement on Technical

---

2   Alan O. Sykes, "Regulatory Protectionism and the Law of International Trade," (1999) 66 *University of Chicago L. Rev.* 1.

3   See Tracey D. Epps, "Reconciling Public Opinion and WTO Rules Under the SPS Agreement," (2008) 7:2 *World Trade Review* 359.

4   See e.g., On Amir and Orly Lobel, "Stumble, Predict, Nudge: How Behavioral Economics Informs Law and Policy," (2008) 108 *Columbia L. Rev.* 2098; Christine Jolls, Cass R. Sunstein, and Richard Thaler, "A Behavioral Approach to Law and Economics," (1998) 50 *Stanford L. Rev.* 147.

5   See Tracey D. Epps and Michael J. Trebilcock, "Import Safety Regulation and International Trade," in Coglianese, Finkel, and Zaring (eds.), *Import Safety, supra* note 1.

Barriers to Trade (often referred to as the Standards Code) was adopted. This was a plurilateral agreement signed by 46 members and while it covered both agricultural and industrial products, it was widely thought deficient in failing to distinguish adequately between "necessary" and "unnecessary" restrictions on trade. Thus, during the Uruguay Round two new agreements were negotiated: the Agreement on Sanitary and Phyto-sanitary Measures (SPS Agreement) and the Technical Barriers to Trade Agreement (TBT Agreement), which are binding on all members. Before reviewing these Agreements, a brief discussion of GATT case-law relating to health and safety regulation is in order.

B.   The GATT Case Law

In the *Thai – Cigarette* case (1990),[6] the U.S. challenged a ban on imports of cigarettes into Thailand as a violation of Article XI of the GATT. Thailand defended the ban under Article XX(b) as necessary for the protection of public health. While no comparable ban existed on domestic Thai cigarettes, the Thai government claimed that American imports were more likely to induce women and young persons to take up smoking, because of sophisticated advertising directed at these groups. The panel ruled that an import ban would only be "necessary" for public health reasons, within the meaning of Article XX(b), if alternative non-trade restricting measures were not available to achieve the public health objectives in question. The panel considered that restrictions or bans on advertising, and labelling and content requirements that applied in a non-discriminatory basis to both domestic cigarettes and imports would be satisfactory alternatives to an import ban, and therefore the ban could not be justified under Article XX(b).

The *EC – Asbestos* case (2000),[7] while post the creation of the WTO, was resolved under the general GATT provisions, after a WTO panel had held (perversely) that a product ban could not be a technical regulation or standard requiring a review under the TBT Agreement. In this case, a French prohibition on the sale or

---

[6]   *Thailand – Restrictions on Importation of and Internal Taxes on Cigarettes* (1990) DS10/R – 37S/200.

[7]   *European Communities – Measures Affecting Asbestos and Asbestos-Containing Products* (2000) WT/DS135/R.

importation of asbestos or products (such as cement) containing asbestos was challenged by Canada. The WTO Panel found that asbestos and PCG fibres (e.g., cellulose and glass fibres, which were not banned) were like products and hence the ban on the former was a breach of Article III.4 (the National Treatment Principle), although the Panel went on to hold that the measure was justified under Article XX(b). The Appellate Body was critical of the Panel for looking exclusively at overlapping end-uses under Article III(4), and even then not the extent of these overlaps. According to the Appellate Body the Panel should have examined all four factors enumerated in the Border Tax Adjustment Working Group Report in 1970: a) physical properties; b) end uses; c) consumer preferences; and d) tariff classification. All four factors bear on the competitive relationship in the marketplace between allegedly like products. In this case, differences in the physical properties of asbestos and PCG fibres were critical – one was carcinogenic and the others not. This raised a strong presumption against the two classes of products being like products.

Like the Panel, the Appellate Body also held that the measure was justified under Article XX(b) and was not satisfied that any alternative measure, such as "controlled use" requirements, were available which France could reasonably be expected to employ to achieve its health and safety policy objectives, which in this case was zero health risk from exposure to asbestos. The Appellate Body in interpreting and applying Article XX(b) suggested that there may be different levels of scrutiny applicable to the analysis of whether a measure is "necessary" depending on the importance of the objectives or interests it serves. In a case such as the present, where the objective pursued by the measure is the preservation of human life and health, and the country's objective is to reduce the health risks in question to zero, the measure is entitled to a "margin of appreciation", and the availability of alternative, less trade-restrictive measures that may not achieve this objective as fully would not disqualify the measure from exemption under Article XX(b).

The recent *Brazil – Tyres* (2007)[8] case reaffirms and extends the analysis in Article XX(b) by the Appellate body in *Asbestos*. *Brazil*

---

    [8]   *Brazil – Measures Affecting Imports of Retreaded Tyres*, 3 December (2007) WT/DS332/AB/R (07-5290).

– *Tyres* can be alternatively thought of as implicating health and safety or environmental issues. In this case, the E.U. challenged a Brazilian import ban on used and retreaded tyres. The justification offered by Brazil for this ban was that, along with other policies, it was designed to reduce the volume of waste tyres, which were a breeding ground for mosquitoes that carried malaria and dengue fever, and moreover that large quantities of waste tyres raised health risks from tyre fires that generated toxic fumes and residue.

Brazil conceded that the ban was a violation of Article XI but sought to justify the ban under Article XX(b). The Appellate Body, upholding the decision of the Panel in these proceedings, interpreted the "necessity" test under Article XX(b) as requiring that the measure in question make a "material contribution" to the achievement of the health and safety objectives in question. A contribution to the achievement of health and safety objectives under Article XX(b) exists when there is a genuine relationship of ends and means between the objective pursued and the measure at issue. To be characterized as necessary, a measure does not have to be indispensable. However, its "contribution to the achievement of the objective must be material, not merely marginal or insignificant, especially if the measure at issue is as trade-restrictive as an import ban. Thus, the contribution of the measure has to be weighed against its trade restrictiveness, taking into account the importance of the interests or the values underlying the objective pursued by it." This is, in effect, a proportionality test or qualitative cost-benefit test.[9]

With respect to the issue of whether less trade-restrictive alternatives might have been available to achieve these objectives, the Appellate Body, again affirming the Panel, held that the E.U. bore the burden of identifying such alternatives, and that the alternatives the E.U. had identified, such as stockpiling and incineration, on the evidence before the Panel, were not as likely to achieve Brazil's health, safety and environmental objectives as the measures it had adopted.

However, turning to the conditions in the chapeau, the Appellate Body overturned two determinations of the Panel in these proceedings. By virtue of a ruling by a MERCOSUR tribunal, following

---

[9] See Alan O. Sykes, "The Least Restrictive Means," (2003) 70:1 *U. of Chicago L. Rev.* 403.

a complaint initiated by Uruguay, the Brazilian ban was held to violate its Mercosur obligations to other Mercosur members, and hence Brazil had begun permitting imports of retreaded tyres from other Mercosur countries, including retreaded tyres originating outside of the Mercosur countries. The Appellate Body held that this was unjustifiably discriminatory towards imports of retreaded tyres from the complainant (the E.U.). In addition, by virtue of injunctions issued by Brazilian courts at the instance of Brazilian tyre retreaders, imports of used tyres by Brazilian retreaders were being permitted by the Brazilian authorities, again in the Appellate Body's view discriminating unjustifiably against imports of retreaded tyres from the E.U.

III. THE SPS AND TBT AGREEMENTS

A. The SPS Agreement[10]

SPS measures include measures applied to protect animal or plant life or health within a territory of a member from risks arising from the entry, establishment or spread of pests, diseases, disease-carrying organisms or disease-causing organisms; and to protect human or animal life or health within the territory of the member from risks arising from additives, contaminants, toxins or disease-causing organisms in foods, beverages or feedstuffs.

Members shall ensure that any SPS measure is applied only to the extent necessary to protect human, animal or plant life or health, is based on scientific principles and is not maintained without sufficient scientific evidence, except as provided for in Article 5.7 (Article 2.2). Members shall ensure that their SPS measures do not arbitrarily or unjustifiably discriminate between members where identical or similar conditions prevail, including between their own territory and that of other members. SPS measures shall not be applied in a manner which would constitute a disguised restriction on international trade (Article 2.3).

SPS measures which conform to international standards,

---

[10] See generally, Tracey D. Epps, *International Trade and Health Protection: A Critical Assessment of the WTO's SPS Agreement* (Cheltenham: Edward Elgar, 2008).

guidelines or recommendations shall be presumed to be consistent with the provisions of this Agreement (Article 3.2). Members may introduce or maintain SPS measures which result in a higher level of SPS protection than would be achieved by measures based on the relevant international standards, guidelines or recommendations, if there is a scientific justification, or as a consequence of the level of SPS protection a member determines to be appropriate in accordance with Article 5.1 to 5.8 (Article 3.3). In such cases, members shall ensure that their SPS measures are based on an assessment, as appropriate to the circumstances, of the risks to human, animal or plant life or health, taking into account risk assessment techniques developed by the relevant international organizations (Article 5.1). Each member shall avoid arbitrary or unjustifiable distinctions in the levels of SPS protection it considers to be appropriate in different situations, if such distinctions result in discrimination or a disguised restriction on international trade (Article 5.5). When establishing or maintaining SPS measures to achieve the appropriate level of SPS protection, members shall ensure that such measures are not more trade-restrictive than required to achieve their appropriate level of SPS protection, taking into account technical and economic feasibility (Article 5.6). For purposes of this article, a footnote to the Agreement provides that a measure is not more trade-restrictive than required unless there is another measure, reasonably available taking into account technical and economic feasibility, that achieves the appropriate level of SPS protection and is significantly less restrictive to trade. When a member has reason to believe that a specific SPS measure introduced or maintained by another member constrains or has the potential to constrain its exports and the measure is not based on relevant international standards, an explanation of the reasons for such an SPS measure may be requested and shall be provided by the member maintaining the measure (Article 5.8).

In cases where relevant scientific evidence is insufficient, a member may provisionally adopt SPS measures on the basis of available pertinent information. In such circumstances, members shall seek to obtain the additional information necessary for a more objective assessment of risk and review the SPS measure accordingly within a reasonable period of time (Article 5.7).

Members shall accept the SPS measures of other members as equivalent if the exporting member objectively demonstrates to the importing member that its measures achieve the importing member's appropriate level of SPS protection. For this purpose, reasonable access shall be given, upon request, to the importing member for inspection, testing and other relevant procedures. Members shall, upon request, enter into consultations with the aim of achieving bilateral and multilateral agreements on recognition of the equivalence of specified SPS measures (Article 4).

The provisions of the SPS Agreement (as with the TBT Agreement) are subject to the general WTO dispute-settlement regime.

B.   TBT Agreement

The TBT Agreement covers all technical product regulations and standards not covered by the SPS Agreement.

Article 2.2 places an obligation on members to ensure that technical regulations are not more trade-restrictive than necessary to fulfill a legitimate objective. The burden of proof is on the complainant to show that a less trade-restricting alternative measure is available. Article 2.2 also states that this obligation not to make technical regulations more trade-restrictive than necessary must take into account the risks that non-fulfillment of the regulatory goal would create. This implies that the length to which a member should be expected to go in exhausting all regulatory alternatives to find the least trade-restricting one is connected to the kind of risk that is being regulated.

Article 2.4 stipulates that, where they exist, members shall use relevant international technical standards as the basis for their own technical regulations, except where such international standards would be an ineffective or inappropriate means for the fulfillment of the legitimate objectives pursued, due to factors such as climate, geography, or technological inability. Unlike the SPS Agreement, "international standards" is not a defined term in the TBT Agreement and there is no list of international standard-setting bodies whose standards are recognized for the purposes of Article 2.4.

Other important provisions under the TBT Agreement include: Article 2.7, which states that members shall give consideration to accepting the technical regulations of other countries as equivalent to their own, provided that the foreign regulations accomplish the same objectives as their own regulations; Article 2.8, which instructs members to design regulations based on product requirements in terms of performance rather than design or descriptive elements; and

Articles 2.5, 2.9, and 2.11, which together impose notification and publication requirements on members enacting new technical regulations, and also require publication in accessible format of existing technical regulations. An Annex to the Agreement contains a Code of Good Practice for the Preparation, Adoption, and Application of Standards which domestic standardizing bodies are expected to adhere to.

The substantive obligations in the SPS and TBT Agreements differ in important ways. For example, Article 2.1 of the TBT Agreement contains a strict prohibition on discrimination, asserting that in respect of technical regulations, members must accord imported products treatment no less favorable than domestic products. In contrast, Article 2.3 of the SPS Agreement acknowledges that discrimination between like products may occur, prohibiting only measures that arbitrarily or unjustifiably discriminate between members where identical or similar conditions prevail.

However, the requirements for scientific evidence are much more stringent under the SPS Agreement. Article 2.2 of the TBT Agreement requires only that scientific information be "considered" as part of the risk-assessment process that leads to national technical standards. In contrast, the SPS Agreement is premised on the notion that requiring scientific justification for standards that deviate from international norms will make it more difficult for members to engage in regulatory protectionism.

C.   The TBT and SPS Case Law

The leading Appellate Body decision on the TBT Agreement is *European Community – Trade Description of Sardines*.[11] In this case Peru challenged a regulation adopted by the European Communities that provided that only products prepared from a certain sub-species of sardines found around the coasts of the eastern North Atlantic, the Mediterranean, and the Black Sea may be marketed as preserved sardines. Only products of this species were permitted to have the word "sardines" as part of the name on the container. Peru argued that this regulation violated Article 2.4 of the TBT Agreement,

---

[11]   *European Community – Trade Description of Sardines* (2002) WT/DS231/AB/R.

which requires that relevant international standards shall be used as a basis for technical regulations except when such international standards or relevant parts would be an ineffective or inappropriate means for the fulfillment of the legitimate objectives pursued. In this case, a standard adopted by the Codex Alimentarius Commission provided that canned sardines could be marketed in accordance with specific labelling provisions using the name "sardines" and including sub-species of sardines other than that to which the E.C. regulation was restricted and which were found mainly in the eastern Pacific along the coasts of Peru and Chile. The Appellate Body held that the E.C. regulation was not based on relevant international standards and that Peru had met the burden of proof of demonstrating that the international standard would be effective in accomplishing all three of the objectives advanced for the E.C. measure – market transparency, consumer protection, and fair competition.

The SPS Agreement to date has attracted much more formal dispute-settlement activity than the TBT Agreement. The leading case is *Beef Hormones* (1998)[12] which concerned a European ban on the sale of beef from animals that had been treated with growth hormones, a practice which was widespread in the United States (and Canada) but not in Europe. Thus, the ban had a significant effect on U.S. beef producers, who either could not sell their beef in Europe or had to take expensive measures to ensure that it was hormone-free, while having little effect on European producers. The United States argued that the ban was disguised protectionism, whereas the European Union maintained that the ban was a legitimate public health measure designed to protect its citizens from possible health risks associated with the presence of hormones in beef. The Appellate Body upheld the U.S. complaint, holding that the E.U.'s regulatory measures did not conform to international standards and were not based on a risk assessment consistent with its WTO obligations.

However, the Appellate Body held that non-conformity with international standards does not create a reverse onus of proof on the respondent to prove compliance with the alternative risk assessment procedures contemplated in Article 5. The burden of proof of non-compliance rests on the complainant. The Appellate Body

---

[12] *EC Measures Concerning Meat and Meat Products* (1998) WT/DS26/AB/R, WT/DS48/AB/R [*Beef Hormones* 1998].

endorsed an approach of examining whether the scientific evidence was "reasonably sufficient" to justify the SPS measure in question.[13] As well, the Appellate Body rejected the existence of any minimum procedural requirements for domestic risk assessment.[14] Thus, it is not necessary for a member who enacts an SPS measure to conduct an investigation, engage in formal fact-finding, or publish a report justifying the SPS measure, and may rely, by way of justification, on risk assessments conducted by other countries or organizations. The Appellate Body held that in the presence of scientific controversy or disagreement, a member may base an SPS measure upon minority, as opposed to mainstream, scientific opinion, provided that the minority opinion comes from "qualified and respected sources".[15] The Appellate Body declined to take a position on whether the precautionary principle has evolved into a principle of customary international law (as the E.U. urged). However, it noted that Article 5.7 that permits countries to adopt provisional measures where there is insufficient scientific evidence to conduct risk assessments, and that Article 3.3, which recognizes the right of countries to establish their own appropriate level of sanitary protection, permits governments to act from perspectives of prudence and caution where risks of irreversible damage to human health are concerned. With respect to the consistency requirement under Article 5.5, the Appellate Body held that closely comparable risks were required in order to evaluate regulatory consistency and that independent proof of discrimination or a disguised restriction on international trade was required (a form of "aims-and-effects" test).

Thus, in the *Beef Hormones* case the Appellate Body adopted a relatively deferential approach to its review of domestic evidence relied on by the respondent to support contested measures. However, the E.U. was unable to satisfy even this standard of review in this case, being unable to point to any scientific risk assessment that supported its position.

In the *Japan – Apples*[16] case the Appellate Body struck a less deferential posture, holding that an assessment of the "rational

---

[13]   *Ibid.* at para. 198.
[14]   *Ibid.* at para. 189.
[15]   *Ibid.* at para. 194.
[16]   *Japan – Measures Affecting the Importation of Apples*, (2003) WT/DS245/AB/R, paras. 160–67.

connection" between scientific evidence and the impugned SPS measure did not require deference to the authorities of the regulating member. However, more recently again, the Appellate Body in further dispute-settlement proceedings in *Beef Hormones* (2008), after the E.U. had undertaken a new risk assessment, sharply criticized the Panel in these proceedings for "somewhat peremptorily" deciding what it considered the best science from its review of expert scientific opinion, rather than the more limited exercise of determining whether the member's risk assessment "is supported by coherent reasoning and respectable scientific evidence and is, in this sense, objectively justifiable".[17]

In another recent case, *Australia – Measures Affecting the Importation of Apples from New Zealand*,[18] the Appellate Body upheld a complaint by New Zealand that various measures adopted by Australia that essentially banned the importation of New Zealand apples failed to satisfy the requirements under Articles 5.1 and 5.2 of the SPS Agreement that such measures be based on a scientific risk assessment. The Appellate Body concluded that the Panel in the case was correct in requiring that the risk assessment base its conclusions, including those reached through expert judgment, on the available scientific evidence and also agreed with the Panel that the risk assessment's use of expert judgment had not been sufficiently documented or transparent and therefore did not constitute a proper risk assessment within the meaning of Articles 5.1 and 5.2. With respect to New Zealand's claim that alternative measures would achieve Australia's appropriate level of protection under Article 5.6 (e.g., the restriction of imports to mature, symptomless apples or sampling requirements for each import lot), the Appellate Body held that a Panel is required to undertake its own analysis as to whether the alternative measures proposed by New Zealand would achieve Australia's appropriate level of protection and that the Panel had wrongly imported reasoning in findings relating to deficiencies in the risk assessment from its analysis of New Zealand's Article 5.1 claim, rather than undertaking an independent analysis of the Article 5.6 claim. The Appellate Body concluded that there were insufficient uncontested

---

[17] *US – Continued Retaliation in the Hormones Dispute* (2008) WT/DS320/R [*U.S. – Continued Suspension*].

[18] *Australia – Measures Affecting the Importation of Apples from New Zealand* (2010) WT/DS367/AB/R.

facts or factual findings to enable it to make a finding on the level of risk associated with New Zealand's alternative measures and therefore could not complete the legal analysis with respect to Article 5.6.

Article 5.7 allows a member to maintain a provisional SPS measure, notwithstanding the requirements of Article 2.2. The Appellate Body has set out four criteria that must be met for a provisional measure to be maintained under Article 5.7: (a) the relevant scientific information is insufficient; (b) the measure is adopted on the basis of pertinent available information; (c) the member adopting the measure is seeking to obtain the additional information necessary for a more objective assessment of the risk; and (d) the member adopting the measure will review it within a reasonable period of time.[19]

A recent Ruling by a WTO Panel in *E.C. – Biotech* appears to shed some additional light on Article 5.7.[20] In this dispute, the complainants (the United States, Canada, and Argentina) challenged the E.C.'s regulatory scheme for the approval of genetically modified organisms (GMO). Among other things,[21] the Panel found that specific E.C. country bans on certain GMO crops did not meet the requirements of Article 5.7 of the SPS. Although Article 5.7 does permit members to adopt provisional measures where there is insufficient scientific evidence to assess the risk, the Panel found that studies carried out on the banned GMO crops by the E.C. scientific committee and by other competent national authorities, which concluded that the GMO crops were safe, constituted sufficient risk assessments under the SPS Agreement. Therefore, the first branch of the test set out for Article 5.7, that there be insufficient scientific information, was not met. Consequently, the Panel recommended that the ban on certain GMO crops be removed.

---

[19] *Japan – Measures Affecting Agricultural Products* (1999) WT/DS76/AB/R, paras. 86–9.
[20] *EC – Measures Affecting the Approval and Marketing of Biotech Products* (2006) WT/DS291, 292, 293/INTERIM.
[21] The Panel also found that the E.C., by applying a de facto moratorium on the approval of new GMO products and failing to consider specific GMOs for approval, had acted inconsistently with Annex C(1)(a) of the SPS Agreement, which requires members to complete testing and approval procedures without undue delay.

IV. CONCLUSION

The Appellate Body of the WTO has generally steered a prudent middle course between complete deference to domestic regulatory authorities in setting health and safety standards that may have adverse impacts on international trade and encouraging panels to engage in a complete, *de novo* review of the scientific evidence relied on to justify such standards (acting as a *de facto* World Science Court).[22] However, with the dramatic growth in imported consumer products, including food products, in many countries over recent years, the fault-lines between consumer and producer (domestic and foreign) interests, and between developing and developed countries are likely to yield a continuing stream of high-profile disputes for resolution by the WTO's Dispute Settlement Body.[23]

---

[22] See Michael J. Trebilcock and Julie A. Soloway, "International Trade Policy and Domestic Food Safety Regulation: The Case for Substantial Deference," in Daniel Kennedy and James Southwick (eds.), *The Political Economy of International Trade: Essays in Honor of Robert E. Hudec* (Cambridge University Press, 2002).

[23] See Coglianese, Finkel, and Zaring, *supra* note 1.

14. Trade policy and the environment

I. INTRODUCTION

The relationship between trade policy and the environment is one of the most controversial issues on the current trade policy agenda, brought into particularly sharp focus by climate change policies currently under consideration in some developed countries that would impose on imports at the border similar burdens, in terms of carbon taxes or emission trading allowances, to those imposed on domestic industries.[1] Two very different classes of claims are made for linking trade policy and environmental concerns.

One class of claim emphasizes the cross-border nature of many environmental problems that entail negative externalities beyond any given jurisdiction. In some cases these concerns implicate the global environmental commons, including the impact of greenhouse gas emissions on climate change; in other cases, shared natural resources or common water or air bodies that straddle the boundaries of more than one jurisdiction. In all these cases, effective environmental regulation ideally requires cooperation amongst all member countries affected by the environmental concern in question. In some cases, trade sanctions, such as a ban on imports, can be seen as a way of enforcing compliance with multilateral environmental agreements (MEAs); in other cases, as inducing non-members to become signatories to such agreements; and in yet other cases, as providing the impetus for the negotiation of such an agreement in the first place.

With this class of claim, it is important to evaluate the likely efficacy of trade sanctions in achieving their intended objective:

[1] See generally, Richard H. Steinberg, "Power and Cooperation in International Environmental Law," in Guzman and Sykes (eds.), *Research Handbook in International Economic Law*, *supra* Chapter 2, note 2.

the empirical evidence suggests that trade sanctions are effective in about one-third of all cases and are likely to be more effective where large countries invoke them against small countries; where policy modifications required are reasonably modest and do not entail full-scale political regime change; and where countries imposing such sanctions and countries targeted by such sanctions generally enjoy workable relationships.[2]

The second class of claim for linking trade policy and environmental concerns is not directly concerned with enhancing environmental protection per se, but levelling the competitive playing field. Here it is argued that it is unfair that firms and workers in countries that have imposed stringent environmental standards should have to bear the burden of these standards through loss of market share to foreign producers who face less stringent standards in their home jurisdictions. In turn, it is argued that it is unfair for countries with lax environmental standards to exert downward pressure, through trade, on the more stringent environmental standards in other countries, hence risking precipitating a race to the bottom. This kind of claim often leads to arguments for equalizing regulatory compliance costs through the imposition of restrictions or duties on imports, whether or not these lead to more stringent environmental standards in exporting countries. Since all kinds of costs vary amongst countries, it is not clear why differences in environmental regulatory compliance costs per se, at least in the absence of jurisdictional environmental externalities, warrant special treatment.

While none of the GATT/WTO agreements contain detailed provisions on the relationship between trade policy and the environment, Article XX of the GATT permits countries to adopt measures "necessary to protect, animal or plant life or health" (Article XX(b)), or "relating to the conservation of exhaustible natural resources if such measures are made effective in conjunction with restrictions on domestic production or consumption" (Article XX(g)), provided that these measures are not applied in a manner which would constitute a means of arbitrary or unjustifiable discrimination, or a disguised restriction on international trade. The Preamble to the Agreement establishing the World Trade Organization refers to "allowing for

---

[2]   See Gary C. Hufbauer, Jeffrey J. Schott and Kimberly A. Elliott, *Economic Sanctions Reconsidered: History and Current Policy* (Washington, DC: Institute for International Economics, 2nd edn., 1990).

the optimal use of the world's resources in accordance with the objective of sustainable development, seeking both to protect and preserve the environment and to enhance the means for doing so in a manner consistent with [members'] respective needs and concerns at different levels of economic development." A number of high profile trade and environment disputes have engaged the formal dispute settlement regime of the GATT/WTO over recent years.

II. OVERVIEW OF GATT/WTO CASE LAW

In one of the first cases involving the relationship between trade policy and the environment to come before a GATT Panel, the *Tuna – Dolphin* case (1991),[3] the U.S. had imposed an embargo on imports of tuna caught by fishing methods that endangered dolphins. The U.S. had banned the use of such fishing techniques in the case of its own fishing fleet. Mexico complained that this embargo violated Article XI of the GATT. The GATT Panel upheld Mexico's complaint, finding a violation of Article XI, and rejecting the application of either Article XX(b) or (g), on the grounds that these two exceptions only applied to health, safety or conservation concerns arising within the territorial jurisdiction of the country seeking to justify trade restrictions and could not be invoked with respect to environmental concerns lying outside such jurisdiction. A second *Tuna – Dolphin* case (1994)[4] involved an E.U. challenge to a secondary embargo in the U.S. legislation aimed at the transshipment of dolphin-unfriendly tuna through a third country that had not adopted a primary embargo of its own. In this case, the GATT Panel accepted that a state could justify trade restrictions under Article XX with respect to environmental concerns beyond its territorial limits, but not if the sole environmental impact of such restrictions sought to be achieved would be through inducing other countries to change their policies. According to the Panel, if Article XX were interpreted to permit members to take trade measures so as to force other members to change their policies within their own jurisdictions, including their environmental policies, rights of access

---

[3] *United States – Restrictions on Imports of Tuna* (1991) DS21/R – 39S/155.

[4] *United States – Restrictions on Imports of Tuna* (1994) DS29/R.

to markets would be seriously impaired, as exporting countries may face multiple and conflicting pre-conditions to such access.

In the first post-1995 WTO case implicating trade and environment issues, *Reformulated Gasoline* (1996),[5] Brazil and Venezuela challenged requirements in regulations under the U.S. Clean Air Act to reduce pollutants in gasoline on a specified time schedule with a 1990 baseline set on a refinery specific basis for U.S. refiners, but in the case of foreign refiners set on the basis of the constructed average 1990 U.S. quality baseline. In this case, the Appellate Body emphasized that the appropriate approach to interpreting and applying Article XX was a two-tiered approach pursuant to which, firstly, the measure in question was evaluated for consistency with one or more of the exceptions enumerated in Article XX, and then second, to evaluate whether the measure in question was being applied in such a way as to violate one or more of the conditions in the chapeau. In this case, the Appellate Body found that the measures in question fell within Article XX(g) and XX(b) but were being applied in a way that was unjustifiably discriminatory towards foreign refiners, and rejected arguments by the U.S. that verification and compliance in the case of foreign refineries with an individual refinery baseline could be administratively burdensome, pointing out that the U.S. had apparently made no attempt to enter into cooperative arrangements with foreign authorities.

However, the leading WTO Appellate Body decision on the relationship between trade and the environment to date is undoubtedly the *Shrimp – Turtles* case,[6] initially decided in 1998 by the Appellate Body and then subsequently revisited in Article 21.5 Compliance Proceedings in 2002.[7] In this case, several Asian countries complained against a U.S. ban on imports of shrimp from countries that had not adopted a comparable regulatory regime to that in place in the U.S., which required shrimp trawlers to install and employ turtle excluder devices (TEDs) in fishing for shrimp in waters where certain

---

[5] *United States – Standards for Reformulated and Conventional Gasoline* (1996) WT/DS2/R.

[6] *United States – Import Prohibition of Certain Shrimp and Shrimp Products* (1998) WT/DS58/AB/R.

[7] *United States – Import Prohibition of Certain Shrimp and Shrimp Products: Recourse to Article 21.5 of the DSU by Malaysia* (2001) WT/DS58/AB/RW.

rare species of sea turtles, listed on a Schedule to the Convention Against International Trade in Endangered Species (CITES), were known to be present. The U.S. conceded that the ban was a violation of Article XI but sought to justify it under Article XX(g). In this case, the WTO Panel, contrary to the approach adopted by the Appellate Body in *Reformulated Gasoline*, started with the chapeau to Article XX and found that the kind of measures in question were inconsistent with the purposes of the GATT and WTO Agreements and were likely to destabilize the multilateral trading system by confronting exporters with multiple compliance preconditions for accessing foreign markets. Given this approach, the Panel never reached the exceptions to Article XX.

The Appellate Body overruled the Panel in this respect and re-emphasized the importance of the two-tiered approach that it had adopted in *Reformulated Gasoline*, in which the first line of inquiry is whether the measure in question fits within one of the enumerated exceptions to Article XX. The Appellate Body emphasized that there was no inherent territorial limitation on the scope of the exceptions enumerated in Article XX. The Appellate Body also held that the concept of "exhaustible natural resources" in Article XX(g) was not restricted to minerals and non-reproducible things, but extended to living things, citing various environmental and conservation treaties to this effect. As to the meaning of "relating to" in Article XX(g), the Appellate Body held that the means adopted in the measure in question should be reasonably related to the ends sought to be achieved, hence implying a kind of proportionality test. In addition, Article XX(g) requires that the measures be made effective in conjunction with restrictions on domestic production or consumption, which in this case was a requirement that the U.S. had clearly satisfied by imposing similar measures on its own fishing fleet.

The Appellate Body then turned to the conditions in the chapeau, whereby measures that are provisionally justified under one of the exceptions to Article XX must not be applied in a manner that would constitute a means of arbitrary or unjustifiable discrimination between countries where the same conditions prevail or a disguised restriction on international trade. The Appellate Body held that these conditions reflected a need to maintain a balance of rights and obligations amongst members so that exceptions did not overwhelm more general obligations, or the reverse. The Appellate Body viewed the conditions in the chapeau as implying a principle of good faith or abuse of rights and the drawing of an "equilibrium line" between when a member may invoke exceptions and when other members may insist on enforcement of obligations owed to them.

In this case, the Appellate Body held that the U.S. measures were being applied in a manner that was unjustifiably discriminatory in that all exporting countries were required to adopt essentially the same policy applied by the U.S. to its own shrimp trawlers and took no account of the circumstances of members who might be differently situated and might be able to achieve comparable levels of effectiveness to the U.S. requirements through other policies. The Appellate Body was also critical of the U.S. for failing to engage in serious across-the-board bilateral or multilateral negotiations with all affected countries, despite directions to this effect in the U.S. statute in question. The Appellate Body emphasized that for cross-border environmental issues, a number of recent environmental treaties and declarations had emphasized the importance of avoiding unilateral measures, if possible, and noted that the U.S. had indeed signed a convention with five countries in Latin America with respect to shrimp exports that provided them with more latitude in various respects as to how to meet U.S. objectives than in the case of the Asian country complainants. Finally, the Appellate Body was also critical of the lack of transparency in the certification processes employed by the U.S. agencies in question where there were no formal opportunities for countries to be heard during the certification process or to be apprised of potential objections to their certification, nor were reasons given for decisions denying certification.

Subsequent to this decision, the U.S. amended its Guidelines, substituting a requirement for a comparably effective regulatory program in order to qualify for certification and rendering more transparent the certification process by providing for notification of potential concerns to countries seeking certification and providing them with an opportunity of reply. Despite these changes, Malaysia argued in Article 21.5 Compliance proceedings that the U.S. was still not non-compliant with its GATT/WTO obligations. While the U.S. had embarked on a series of steps designed to yield consensus on an international agreement with respect to shrimp fishing in the South East Asian region, Malaysia argued that the U.S. was not only under a duty to negotiate but in fact to conclude an international agreement. The Appellate Body rejected this argument, pointing out that this would give exporting countries a veto over a right of an importing country to invoke trade restrictions that would otherwise fall within one of the Article XX exceptions, and thus negate such exceptions. The Appellate Body accepted that there was evidence of recent good faith efforts by the U.S. to negotiate an agreement with Southeast Asian countries and that the revised Guidelines were sufficiently flexible to accommodate different policies that would achieve comparable levels of effectiveness with the policies that the U.S. had imposed on its own fishing trawlers.

In many respects the cumulative effect of the two Appellate Body decisions in *Shrimp – Turtles* (along with its recent decision in *Brazil – Tyres*,[8] discussed in the previous chapter) is largely to overturn the two earlier GATT Panel decisions in the *Tuna – Dolphin* cases and to establish a more sensitive balance between trade and environmental concerns.

III. TRADE POLICY AND CLIMATE CHANGE[9]

As noted at the outset of this chapter, a number of developed countries, including the U.S. and the E.U., are actively considering imposing on imports of goods carbon tariffs or emission allowance requirements comparable to those imposed on their own domestic producers of like products. These proposals have already begun to generate intense controversy in international trade circles and are seen by some developing countries, on the one hand, as an attempt to force on them greenhouse gas abatement policies comparable to those in place in developed countries, notwithstanding the fact that developed countries are responsible for most of the effects of greenhouse gas emissions on climate change that have occurred to date. Developed countries, on the other hand, are concerned that in the absence of such measures, their domestic measures designed to reduce CO_2 emissions will be negated if this means a loss of market share and jobs to firms in developing countries, such as China and India, who might face less stringent requirements. Moreover, developed countries' governments are concerned that their own firms may

---

[8] *Brazil – Measures Affecting Imports of Retreaded Tyres* 2007, *supra* Chapter 13, note 8.
[9] See generally, Andrew Green and Tracey D. Epps, *Reconciling Trade and Climate Change* (Cheltenham: Edward Elgar, 2010).

simply relocate to countries with less stringent regimes, not only negating the abatement objectives of the climate change policies adopted by developed countries, but sacrificing domestic jobs and investment in the process.

While assessing the compatibility of carbon tariffs and like measures with members' GATT/WTO obligations raises a number of complex issues, which are in part a function of the particular design features of the measures in question, certain provisions in the GATT are likely to assume central importance.[10] First, Article II:2 provides that "Members are free to impose at any time on the importation of any product a charge equivalent to an internal tax imposed consistently with provisions of paragraph 2 of Article III in respect of the like domestic product or in respect of an article from which the imported product has been manufactured or produced in whole or in part." A report of the GATT Working Party on Border Tax Adjustments in 1970 sought to clarify the scope of this provision, pointing out that it was largely limited to indirect taxes such as excise taxes, sales taxes, value-added taxes, and not direct taxes, such as income taxes or payroll taxes. In general, Article II:2 has been applied to various kinds of consumption taxes, which are often waived or rebated by exporting countries, and imposed by importing countries, thus avoiding double taxation of imports. As to whether measures equivalent to carbon tariffs would also fall within the scope of Article II:2, in part, turns on whether the tariff or other charge can be viewed as imposed in respect of either the imported product or an article from which the imported product was manufactured, rather than CO_2 emissions generated in the course of its production. Even if permitted, Article II:2 requires that the requirements of Article III.2 of the GATT be satisfied, which embodies the National Treatment Principle as applied to internal taxes, and prohibits charging taxes on imported products in excess of, or dissimilar to, taxes imposed on domestic like products. This non-discrimination requirement implies that any attempt to impose carbon tariffs or similar charges at the border is likely to be closely scrutinized in dispute-settlement proceedings in terms of whether, as designed and applied, it has a differential impact on imports.

---

[10]   See Paul-Erik Veel, "Carbon Tariffs and the WTO: An Evaluation of Feasible Policies," (2009) 12:3 *Journal of International Economic Law* 749.

Even if carbon tariffs or similar measures are unable to satisfy the terms of Article II.2, or violate other provisions of the GATT, for example Article I (Most Favoured Nation) or Article XI (Quantitative Restrictions), the country imposing such measures is likely to seek to justify these measures under Article XX, especially Articles XX(b) and XX(g). It seems likely that such measures can be justified as falling within the scope of one or both of these exceptions, but ensuring that such measures satisfy all the conditions in the chapeau may be more challenging, particularly if some foreign exporting countries are exempted from the measures, while attempts are made to differentiate the burdens imposed on remaining exporting countries reflecting relative abatement efforts undertaken in these countries. These differentiated burdens presumably will require justification so as to avoid characterization as arbitrary or unjustifiable forms of discrimination or disguised restrictions on trade. Government subsidies to promote renewable energy production or to offset costs of retooling conventional production processes to reduce carbon emissions are likely to fall within the ambit of the SCM Agreement (reviewed in Chapter 7), which notably does not contain any equivalent provision to Article XX of the GATT. Government procurement policies relating to the construction of renewable energy facilities, especially local sourcing requirements, are likely to be reviewable under the Government Procurement Agreement for member states that are signatories to this Agreement (or regional agreements, such as the government procurement provisions of NAFTA).

15. Trade policy, labour standards and human rights

I. INTRODUCTION

The idea of using international labour standards to protect workers from economic exploitation was first promoted by individual social reformers in the first half of the nineteenth century in the early stages of the Industrial Revolution. The work of these reformers was taken over by various non-governmental organizations, including various international organizations (in particular, international associations of trade unions) in the second half of the nineteenth century. Inter-governmental actions to promote international labour standards began to be reflected in international conferences beginning in 1890 and culminated in the establishment of the International Labour Organization (ILO) by the Treaty of Versailles in 1919. The ILO, a tripartite organization of government, employers and worker representatives, has mostly pursued its mandate by setting minimum international standards through Conventions and Recommendations, subject in the former case to ratification by member states and promoted by investigation, public reporting and technical assistance, but not formal sanctions. In 1998, the ILO adopted the Declaration of Fundamental Principles and Rights at Work providing that all members have an obligation to respect and promote certain core labour standards (CLS): 1) freedom of association and the right to engage in collective bargaining; 2) the elimination of forced labour; 3) the elimination of child labour; and 4) the elimination of discrimination in employment. This Declaration parallels, in many respects, references to core international labour standards in the UN Universal Declaration of Human Rights (1948), the UN Covenant on Civil and Political Rights, and the UN Covenant on Economic, Social and Cultural Rights that came into force in 1976.[1]

---

[1]   See more generally, Michael J. Trebilcock and Robert Howse, "Trade Policy and Labour Standards," (2005) 14:2 *Minnesota J. of Global Trade*

The 1948 Havana Charter that was intended to embody the framework for a new world trading system also declared that "members recognize that unfair labour conditions, particularly in production for export, create difficulties in international trade and accordingly each member shall take whatever action may be appropriate and feasible to eliminate such conditions within its territory." However, the Havana Charter was never adopted because of opposition in the U.S. Congress, so that the GATT that emerged in 1947 contains few references to labour standards. The Ministerial Declaration following the first WTO Ministerial Conference in Singapore in 1966 appears to have removed labour issues from the WTO agenda and remitted them to the ILO. The 2001 Doha Ministerial Declaration reaffirms this position.

Regional trade agreements such as NAFTA, the U.S.–Jordan Free Trade Agreement, and the U.S.–Cambodia Free Trade Agreement contain provisions requiring signatories to effectively enforce their own labour standards and to strive towards improving and enhancing their existing labour standards. In the case of NAFTA, failure to enforce existing labour standards may lead to formal complaints and determinations by dispute-settlement panels of violations resulting in fines against the offending country which, in the case of the U.S. and Mexico, can be enforced by trade sanctions and in the case of Canada by direct enforcement of the penalty in Canadian courts. These fines are payable to the offending country on condition that they be devoted to enhancing labour standards. Beyond these regional trade agreements, a number of developed countries, most notably the U.S. and the E.U. membership, have often conditioned the granting of preferences to developing countries under their Generalized System of Preference (GSP) programs on conformity with international labour standards. In the case of the E.U., accession negotiations with prospective member states have often entailed insistence on adherence to core labour standards and basic human rights more generally.[2]

261; Christian Barry and Sanjay G. Reddy, *International Trade and Labor Standards: A Proposal for Linkage* (New York: Columbia University Press, 2008).

  [2] See Michael J. Trebilcock and Ronald Daniels, *Rule of Law Reform and Development: Charting the Fragile Path of Progress* (Cheltenham: Edward Elgar, 2008), Chapter 10.

II. RATIONALES FOR A TRADE POLICY–LABOUR STANDARDS–HUMAN RIGHTS LINKAGE

Several rationales for such a linkage have often been advanced. First, it is argued that it is unfair for firms and workers in developed countries to have to compete with firms and workers in developing countries where labour standards and labour costs are much lower, and hence risk losing market share and jobs to these countries. Second, it is argued that this form of competition may lead to a race to the bottom, where countries will be induced to ratchet down their labour standards to the lowest common denominator, but at the end of this process of destructive competition end up with similar market shares (a form of Prisoner's Dilemma or collective action problem). Third, it is often argued that core labour standards should be conceived of as basic human rights as reflected in the UN Universal Declaration of Human Rights and the UN Covenants on Civil and Political Rights and Economic, Social and Cultural Rights.

The first two rationales for a trade policy–labour standards linkage are problematic, in that they focus on social welfare in *importing* countries, rather than on social welfare in *exporting* countries where the allegedly low labour standards prevail. Moreover, objecting to this form of competition carries a serious risk of depriving developing countries of one of their major sources of comparative advantage, that is, low labour costs. However, in this respect, it is important to note that labour costs and labour productivity are closely correlated and, in the case of developing countries, reflect the absence or low quality of many complementary factors of production, such as infrastructure, education and training, managerial expertise, and health care policies. Thus, it would be a mistake to assume that international trade, or foreign direct investment, is mostly driven by differences in labour costs and standards – indeed, international trade and foreign direct investment flows are typically dominated by North–North rather than North–South relationships.

With respect to the third rationale for a trade policy–labour standards linkage, the focus is squarely on social welfare considerations in exporting countries, rather than importing countries, and seems an entirely cogent basis for collective global action to ensure that core labour standards in all countries, conceived of as universal human rights, and other international human rights are respected. Basic universal human rights, while defying precise definition, have increasingly come to be viewed as a fundamental element of customary international law (*Jus Cogens*), and to the extent that they extend beyond particular treaty obligations, are viewed as obligations *Erga Omnes* which are owed to the international community at large and hence are enforceable by all members of that community.

This said, the precise content of several of the core labour standards (and indeed the scope of international human rights more generally) is subject to debate. In the case of labour standards, what forms of child labour are unacceptable; what limits on collective bargaining and the right to strike are acceptable? In addition, adopting a human rights perspective on core labour standards, the trade policy–labour standards linkage is problematic to the extent that it is triggered by the importation of goods from countries where these goods are produced in violation of core labour standards. Many violations of core labour standards occur in non-traded goods sectors (e.g., use of child labour) and hence are likely to escape the reach of trade sanctions by importing countries. Also, conditioning the imposition of such sanctions on the importation of goods produced in circumstances that reflect non-compliance with core labour standards risks protectionist abuse of such sanctions by importing countries, rather than an exclusive focus on the effect of inadequate labour standards on the welfare of citizens in exporting countries. Finally, there is no defensible case for privileging core labour standards over other basic international human rights such as freedom from genocide, torture, arbitrary arrest or detention without trial, or racial or gender discrimination – to do so risks eliding protectionist rationales for a trade policy–labour rights linkage with human rights rationales that are much more congruent with normative conceptions of development.[3]

---

[3] See generally Amartya Sen, *Development as Freedom* (New York: Knopf, 1999).

III. CHOICE OF INSTRUMENT

A. The Enforceability of ILO Conventions

As noted above, the ILO has not historically invoked formal sanctions for violations of its Conventions, although Article 33 of the ILO Constitution can be interpreted as embracing trade sanctions in some circumstances. Critics of the ILO argue that it has been largely ineffective in ensuring adherence to its Conventions, although defenders of the ILO point out that, as a tripartite organization, attaching trade sanctions to violations of its Conventions may destabilize the organization and induce some countries to withdraw from membership or, alternatively, decline to ratify Conventions that may attract trade sanctions for breach.

B. Soft Law Options

A prominent class of soft instruments that has emerged in recent years entails a range of certification, labelling and voluntary code-of-conduct mechanisms that purport to identify firms or products that conform to core international labour standards and to promote corporate social responsibility. The efficacy of these mechanisms turns largely on market reactions to the signals that they entail, principally by consumers in importing countries, and to a lesser extent by investors. "Soft" or voluntary approaches suffer from a number of limitations. Currently, they apply to a small percentage of exports in a number of sectors where non-compliance with core labour standards is thought to be common, and they vary widely in various dimensions, including: 1) which core labour standards are recognized; 2) how these core labour standards are defined, if at all; and 3) how effectively adherence to these standards is monitored, if at all. Moreover, their efficacy largely turns on how consumers, and possibly investors, are likely to react to the information conveyed by these mechanisms. In this respect, the voluntary and decentralized nature of the soft law mechanisms currently employed in this context does little to mitigate the information problems faced by consumers (and investors) in importing countries. Moreover, these mechanisms do not address collective action problems confronting consumers in importing countries who may be prepared to pay a premium for goods produced in conditions that meet core labour standards but will be concerned that other consumers who share their concerns may opportunistically purchase lower-priced goods, relying on other consumers to bear the financial costs of vindicating their collective preferences. However, if every consumer suspects every other consumer of being likely to behave opportunistically, that is, to free-ride on their sacrifices, an effective voluntary collective response may not emerge. Finally, because these mechanisms largely turn on potential consumer responses in importing countries, they are not responsive to abuses of core labour standards or other violations of basic human rights in non-traded goods sectors.

C. Carrots

As noted above, various developed countries have often conditioned GSP preferences, or additional margins of preference, on adherence by developing countries with core labour standards, or other human rights, and there appears to be some evidence that these inducements, at least in some cases, have had positive effects on labour standards and their enforcement in developing countries, although carrots sometimes have the perverse effect of rewarding non-compliance.

D. Sticks

Trade sanctions, for example in the form of bans on imports of goods produced in circumstances that violate core labour standards or other international human rights, have sometimes been invoked. While the efficacy of trade sanctions in changing offending behavior has a mixed record, this record must be compared to other responses, from diplomatic protest notes, on the one hand, to military invasion on the other, which also exhibit mixed records of efficacy. Trade sanctions raise difficult questions under the GATT/ WTO system as it currently exists. For example, conditioning MFN treatment on adherence to core labour standards is likely to raise questions as to whether this form of conditionality violates the requirement of "unconditional" extension of MFN treatment to all GATT/WTO members under Article I of the GATT. Existing case law would appear to rule out conditionality tied to country of origin, but perhaps not other forms of conditionality that are not country-of-origin specific. Similarly, under Article III of the GATT (National Treatment), complex issues are likely to arise as to whether goods produced in exporting countries in circumstances that do not conform to core labour standards are "like" products produced in importing countries that conform to these standards. Moreover, a ban on offending imports may well trigger Article XI of the GATT (Quantitative Restrictions).

In the event that trade sanctions in these circumstances are held to violate Article I, Article III or Article XI, an importing country would be required to justify these measures under Article XX, which for the most part is silent on labour standards, although a cogent argument can be made that the "public morals" exception under Article XX(a), interpreted in a dynamic way, should be viewed as embracing the body of core international labour standards and universal human rights more generally that has evolved in the post-war period. A recent decision by a WTO panel and the Appellate Body in the *Online Gambling* case (2004),[4] in interpreting the public morals-public order exception in Article XIV of GATS, which is analogous to the "public morals" exception in Article XX(a) of the GATT, lends some support for this view.

E. Choice of Institutional Regime

It is far from clear that the WTO, as an international trade organization, can credibly and legitimately serve as the central international institutional locus for resolving concerns over core labour standards or universal human rights more generally. In the case of gross violations of universal human rights, such as genocide, apartheid, torture, and detention without trial, specialized UN organs, including the Security Council in the most egregious cases, and UN Committees on Human Rights, are a more credible locus of institutional responsibility. Similarly, in the case of violations of core labour standards, the ILO clearly has much more expertise and legitimacy than the WTO. These issues of institutional competence and legitimacy would appear to require creative forms of horizontal coordination or linkage between the WTO and other international organizations, particularly in the WTO's dispute-settlement role. For example, where trade sanctions have been invoked against imports from

---

[4] *United States – Measures Affecting the Cross-Border Supply of Gambling and Betting Services* (2004) WT/DS285/R; *U.S. – Gambling* (2005) WT/DS285/AB/R.

foreign countries for failure to observe core labour standards or other universal human rights, and these sanctions have been challenged before the WTO Dispute Settlement Body by exporting countries, it would seem appropriate that the WTO Dispute Settlement Body seek opinions from other international organizations whose mandates squarely embrace these issues about whether systematic violations of core labour standards or universal human rights have occurred or are occurring, leaving the WTO dispute-settlement system to address the proportionality of the proposed sanctions relative to the severity and persistence of the abuses in question and to screen out arbitrary or unjustifiable forms of discrimination or disguised restrictions on trade under the conditions in the chapeau to Article XX.

16. Trade policy and developing countries

I. INTRODUCTION

In terms of external revenues of developing countries, foreign aid accounts for about $100 billion per year, remittances from emigrants about $300 billion, FDI about $500 billion, and exports about $1800 billion. Thus, international trade is of critical importance to developing countries. However, many developing countries face special challenges in competing in an increasingly global economy, leading to early recognition by GATT members that various dispensations were justified in accommodating their needs within the multilateral trading system. These dispensations permit greater scope for restricting imports to promote infant industries or to address balance of payments problems and as a necessary corollary contemplate non-reciprocal trade concessions by developed countries with respect to products of actual or potential export interest to developing countries (often referred to as "special and differential treatment").

A. Special and Differential Treatment

Developing countries played a peripheral role in the formation of the GATT. However, they now dominate numerically the membership of the WTO. A key challenge facing the WTO is how to better integrate developing countries into the multilateral trading system.[1] During the period from 1980–99, developing countries' share of global trade was essentially unchanged – 27.4 per cent in 1980 compared to 28.8 per cent in 1999.[2]

---

[1]   For a history of developing countries in the GATT system, see Robert E. Hudec, *Developing Countries in the GATT Legal System* (London: Gower, 1987).

[2]   Constantine Michaelopoulos, *Developing Countries in the WTO* (New

Article XVIII of the GATT (in the form that emerged after a review of the Agreement in 1954–55) contains detailed provisions regarding developing country members. In large part, these provisions granted developing country members exemptions from their GATT commitments in order to "grant the tariff protection required for the establishment of a particular industry", that is, to promote specific domestic industries through import substitution policies, and to restrict imports in order to address balance of payment difficulties. In 1965, Part IV of the GATT, entitled "Trade and Development" was added. Unlike Article XVIII, which focuses on permitting developing country protectionism, Part IV focuses on expanding developing country access to developed country export markets. The key principle of Part IV was "special and differential treatment", under which developed countries were urged to make tariff concessions to developing countries on a non-reciprocal basis. However, most of the commitments in Part IV are merely hortatory and non-binding on developed country members.

The most substantive measures taken in the GATT to address the plight of developing countries were two waivers adopted in 1971. One waiver provided an exception to the MFN obligation in order to allow developed countries to grant preferential tariff treatment to developing countries (known as the Generalized System of Preferences (GSP)). The second waiver to the MFN principle permitted developing countries to exchange such preferences amongst themselves. These waivers were formalized as a permanent part of the GATT in 1979 through an instrument known as the Enabling Clause.[3] Article 1 authorizes preferential tariff reductions toward developing countries on a "generalized, non-reciprocal and non-discriminatory" basis, providing that notwithstanding the MFN obligation, "contracting parties may accord differential and more favorable treatment to developing countries, without according such treatment to other contracting parties". Under Article 5, such preferential treatment is non-reciprocal: "The developed countries do not

York: Palgrave, 2001) at 7–16, as cited in Mitsuo Matsushita, Thomas J. Schoenbaum, and Petros C. Mavroidis, *The World Trade Organization: Law, Practice, and Policy* (Oxford: Oxford University Press, 2009) at 373.

[3] GATT Contracting Parties Decision of November 28, 1979 on Differential and More Favorable Treatment, Reciprocity and Fuller Participation on Developing Countries (Enabling Clause).

expect reciprocity for commitments made by them in trade negotiations to reduce or remove tariffs and other barriers to the trade of
developing countries. . .". Article 5 is also authority for "special and
differential treatment" for developing countries, providing that in
the course of multilateral trade negotiations, developing countries
shall not be required to make "concessions that are inconsistent with
[their] development, financial, and trade needs". Article 7 is known
as the "graduation clause", which envisions that as developing countries' "capacity to make contributions or negotiated concessions"
increases along with their economic development, they are expected
to "participate more fully in the framework of rights and obligations
under the [GATT]".

Many developed countries have adopted GSP programs which
extend preferential terms of trade to developing countries.[4] However,
these GSP tariffs usually entail escape clause provisions in the event
of import surges, and have not been extended to politically sensitive items such as textiles, clothing, and footwear, even though such
items are often of major export interest to many developing countries. Furthermore, as MFN tariff rates have continued to decline
since the inception of the GSP in the 1970s, the margin of preference
between MFN rates and GSP rates has contracted.

Major issues pertaining to the administration of the GSP system
arose in the *EC – Tariff Preferences* (2004),[5] where India complained
that additional tariff preferences were being offered by the E.U.,
beyond baseline GSP preferences, to a sub-set of developing countries that agreed to certain conditions pertaining to labour standards,
environmental standards, and the war on drugs. In the event, India
chose to focus only on the last of these three conditions (drug trafficking), where additional preferences were extended to a closed list
of 12 countries, without any articulated criteria or any opportunity
for other countries to qualify, short of a change in the relevant E.C.

---

4   Some examples of US legislation include the *Caribbean Basin Trade
Partnership Act*, the *Africa Growth and Opportunity Act*, the *Andean Trade
Preferences Act*. The EU's Cotonou Agreement extends tariff preferences to
a wide range of developing countries. See Matsushita et al., *supra* note 2 at
384.
5   *European Communities – Conditions for Granting of Preferences to
Developing Countries*, 20 September 2004, WT/DS246/R [*EC – Tariff
Preferences* 2004]; (2004) WT/DS246/AB/R.

regulation. India argued that this violated both the unconditionality requirement of Article I of the GATT, and the non-discrimination requirement in the 1979 Enabling Clause. The WTO Panel upheld India's complaints on both grounds. On appeal, the Appellate Body focused only on the terms of the Enabling Clause and held that nondiscriminatory treatment did not require extension of GSP preferences to all developing countries without differentiation or discrimination, but only to developing countries similarly situated in terms of stages of development and financial and economic needs. Thus, developed countries could discriminate amongst developing countries on this basis, although the Appellate Body held that the European Communities' program of additional preferences for some developing countries with particular drug trafficking problems, by virtue of its closed list nature and the absence of articulated qualifying criteria, violated this condition.

Most GATT/WTO agreements contain other forms of "special and differential treatment", entailing less onerous obligations and longer phase-in periods for developing countries. The following is a brief overview of the provisions for special and differential treatment in some GATT/WTO agreements.

B. SCM Agreement

Under Article 27.1 of the SCM Agreement, members recognize that subsidies may play an important role in the economic development programs of developing country members. Thus, Article 27 provides certain exemptions from the SCM Agreement for developing countries. Under Articles 27.2 and 27.3, the prohibitions in Article 3 on export subsidies and subsidies contingent on the use of domestic inputs do not apply to least-developed countries, and other developing countries are given a grace period of five to eight years to comply with this prohibition. A further series of provisions appear to be designed to raise the legal standard that must be met in order to bring a successful subsidies complaint against developing countries, thus reducing the possibility of "trade harassment". With respect to actionable subsidies, the dispute resolution process may not be invoked unless the subsidy entails nullification or impairment of GATT concessions or injury to the complaining party's domestic industry (Article 27.9). Countervailing duty actions may not proceed if a domestic agency determines that the overall level of a subsidy granted by a developing country is less than 2 per cent of the per-unit value, or the subsidizing country has less than 4 per cent market share with respect to the subsidized product in the complaining country (Article 27.10).[6]

Despite the special and differential treatment provided for in the SCM Agreement, developed countries are by far the most frequent initiators of countervailing duty claims, and developing countries are the most frequent targets. Out of the 168 countervailing duty initiations filed with the WTO from its inception in 1996 to 31 December 2003, 120 of those were filed by the European Community, United States, and Canada alone. Developing countries and economies in transition were the target of 110 of these initiations.[7]

C. Government Procurement Agreement

Article V of the GPA provides for special and differential treatment for developing countries. In particular, developing countries may negotiate exclusions from rules on national treatment under the GPA. Developed countries are under an obligation to facilitate increased imports from developing countries, provide government procurement-related technical assistance to developing countries, and respond to reasonable information requests from developing countries in the context of a tendering process.[8]

D. SPS and TBT Agreements

Both the TBT and SPS Agreements contain provisions regarding technical assistance and longer phase-in periods for developing countries. Article 9 of the SPS Agreement provides that technical assistance, for example assistance in developing national regulatory agencies, will be given to developing countries in order to allow them

---

   [6]   The comparable *de minimus* rule for developed countries is 1 per cent of per-unit value. (SCM Article 11.9)

   [7]   Data source: WTO – CV Initiations: By Reporting Member – 01/01/95 – 31/12/03.   Online: http://www.wto.org/english/tratop_e/scm_e.htm. Accessed 12 February 2005.

   [8]   Vinod Rege, "Transparency in Government Procurement: Issues of Concern and Interest to Developing Countries," (2001) 35:4 *Journal of World Trade* at 497.

to achieve the appropriate level of sanitary or phytosanitary protection in their export markets. Article 10.2 of the SPS Agreement states that where developed countries introduce new SPS regulations and there is a phase-in period, longer compliance time-frames should be accorded to products of interest to developing countries. Developing country members are also accorded the possibility of time-limited exceptions in whole or in part from obligations under this Agreement, taking into account their financial, trade, and development needs.

Article 11.8 of the TBT Agreement gives priority to the technical assistance needs of developing countries. Article 12.3 states that technical regulations, standards, and conformity assessment procedures of developed country members should take account of the needs of developing country members, with a view to ensuring that such technical regulations, standards, and conformity assessment procedures do not create unnecessary obstacles to exports from developing country members.

E.   TRIPS Agreement

Developing countries are entitled to a one-year delay in implementing the Agreement and a further four-year delay upon application to the TRIPS Council. A further five-year delay applies where a particular area of technology is currently unprotectable under the domestic law of a developing country. Least-developed countries are exempted entirely from the Agreement for ten years (extended to 2016 in the case of pharmaceutical patent protection by the Doha Declaration on Public Health, November 2001).

F.   The Agreement on Textiles and Clothing

The Multi-Fiber Arrangement (MFA), governing trade in textiles and clothing was formally established in 1974, between nine importing developed countries and 31 exporting developing countries. It limits exports by the developing countries to developed countries, through a variety of special safeguard measures, quotas, and voluntary restrictions. The effect of the MFA on developing countries has been severe. It has been estimated that if *all* trade restrictions on LDC textile and clothing imports were lifted by the E.U., Japan, and the United States, the gains to LDCs would be no less than

50.8 per cent of total possible gains related to trade.[9] The Uruguay Round Agreement on Textiles and Clothing provides for the gradual removal of the quantitative restrictions provided for under the MFA, but still leaves high tariffs in place on many products and is subject to a special safeguards regime.

G. Dispute Settlement Understanding

The Dispute Settlement Understanding (DSU) contains various procedural safeguards designed for the benefit of developing country members. Among them are Article 12.10, which grants developing country members additional time in answering a complaint brought against them, and Article 12.11, which requires panels, where one or more of the parties to a dispute is a developing country, to explicitly indicate the form in which account has been taken of relevant provisions on special and differential treatment for developing country members which have been raised by the developing country member in the course of dispute-settlement procedures. Article 8.10 states that in disputes involving a developing country member and a developed country member, if the developing country member requests, at least one of the panelists must be from a developing country member. Finally, Article 24 requires developed country members to exercise "due restraint" in initiating trade disputes and claims for trade compensation against least-developed country members, and provides for an enhanced mediation process for disputes involving a developing country member before the dispute is referred to a panel.

II. SPECIAL AND DIFFERENTIAL TREATMENT: AN ASSESSMENT

The two limbs of Special and Differential Treatment (SDT) that are sketched above need to be seen as inherently interrelated. The much greater policy flexibility extended to developing countries on the import side necessarily implies that in securing better access

---

[9] Marcelo de Paiva Abreu and Winston Fritsch, "Market Access for Manufactured Exports from Developing Countries: Trends and Prospects," in J. Whalley (ed.), *Developing Countries and the Global Trading System, vol I.* (London: Macmillan, 1989) at 117.

to developed countries' markets for their exports, they cannot be expected to offer reciprocal trade concessions (without undermining their policy flexibility on the import side). Hence the second limb of SDT contemplates non-reciprocal and preferential treatment of exports from developing countries by developed countries. While it was assumed that this combination of policies would substantially enhance the economic prospects of developing countries, this assumption has come under increasingly searching scrutiny in academic research.

A. Import Substitution Policies

Extensive dispensations from GATT disciplines (that can be compendiously characterized as infant industry or import substitution rationales for protectionism) were justified on various grounds. First, it was widely argued by many developing countries, and indeed by many mainstream development economists in developed countries and international agencies in the early years of the GATT, that developing countries had often inherited truncated economies from their colonial overseers, where they had been largely restricted economically to the role of hewers of wood and drawers of water, leaving them with large, traditional and inefficient agricultural sectors where the marginal product of labour was often thought to be negligible or even zero. As with most developed countries earlier in their histories, a major transformation in developing country economies was called for in reallocating resources from traditional agricultural sectors to industrial or manufacturing sectors. To facilitate and encourage this, it was argued that at least temporary protectionism was required for these fledgling manufacturing industries, in order to enable them to achieve minimum efficient scale and become competitive in both domestic and export markets. Second, it was widely argued that infant industry protectionism had been aggressively pursued by many developed countries early in the process of their economic development, including the United States, Canada, Germany, and many other currently developed countries, and that developing countries that found themselves at similar stages of development in their early post-independence histories should not be denied similar policy flexibility. Third, it was often argued that because of low levels of education, poor physical infrastructure, weakly developed financial, credit and insurance markets, and inadequate or nonexistent social safety nets, adjustment costs faced by many developing countries in moving to a fully open international trading regime were likely to prove much more severe than those facing developed countries embarking upon a similar strategy of trade liberalization. Fourth, it was also often argued that, at least for smaller and poorer developing countries, their share of world trade, and in particular imports, was typically so small that protectionist policies on their part were likely to have negligible adverse impacts on world prices in the commodities affected by these policies and hence any terms-of-trade externalities from the pursuit of such policies were likely to be small to nonexistent.

However, much research beginning in the 1960s and increasing through the 1970s has found that import-substitution policies were not achieving their goals and were actually hindering the growth of developing countries.[10] For example, research by Balassa found that protectionist policies had hurt developing countries by encouraging industrialization at the expense of agriculture, worsened income distribution, reduced domestic savings, increased unemployment, and led to a very low rate of capital utilization. Little et al. demonstrated the high and indiscriminate levels of protectionism in many developing countries, and research by Krueger revealed the rise of rent-seeking behaviour and corruption that accompanied highly

---

[10]   See, for example, Ian Little, Tibor Sctivsky and Maurice Scott, *Industry and Trade in Some Developing Countries* (London: Oxford University Press, 1970); Bela Balassa, *The Structure of Protection in Developing Countries* (Baltimore: Johns Hopkins University Press, 1971); Anne O. Krueger, *Foreign Trade Regimes and Economic Development: Liberalization Attempts and Consequences* (Lexington, MA: Ballinger, 1979); and Jagdish N. Bhagwati, *Foreign Trade Regimes and Economic Development: Anatomy and Consequences of Exchange Control Regimes* (Lexington, MA: Ballinger, 1978). Writing in 2001, Jeffrey Williamson reports that the World Bank has conducted over 41 studies of developing countries and contrasted the performance of relatively open and relatively closed economies and concluded that trade openness and growth are positively correlated. See Jeffrey G. Williamson, "Winners and Losers over Two Centuries of Globalization", (2002) World Institute for Development Economics Research Annual Lecture (WIDER) at p. 9. Also see Jeffrey D. Sachs and Andrew Warner, "Economic Reform and the Process of Global Integration", (1995) 26:1 Brookings Papers on Economic Activity 1; and David Dollar, "Outward-Oriented Developing Economies Really Do Grow More Rapidly: Evidence from 95 LDCs, 1976-1985", (1992) 40:3 *Economic Development and Cultural Change* 523.

Table 16.1   *Trade-policy orientation and growth rates in the Third World, 1963–92*

Trade policy orientation	Average annual rates growth of GDP per capita (%)		
	1963–73	1973–85	1985–92
Strongly open to trade	6.9	5.9	6.4
Moderately open	4.9	1.6	2.3
Moderately anti-trade	4.0	1.7	−0.2
Strongly anti-trade	1.6	−0.1	−0.4

discretionary protectionist trade policies and related policies such as foreign exchange controls. More recent scholarship has provided further evidence of the positive relationship between trade openness and growth, stemming from gains from improved resource allocation, greater potential to realize economies of scale, improved access to technology, greater domestic competition, and increased domestic savings and foreign direct investment. While measuring trade openness is not unproblematic, these findings are reflected in Table 16.1 from Williamson.[11]

These findings are often reinforced by reference to the trade policies pursued by the so-called East Asian miracle economies, beginning with Japan in the early post-war years and followed by Hong Kong, Singapore, Taiwan, Korea, Malaysia, Thailand and more recently by Vietnam, China and India, or African countries like Botswana and Mauritius or Latin American countries like Chile. In one respect or another, all these countries have pursued policies of export-led growth, although it must be acknowledged that there is ongoing, and to some extent unresolved, controversy as to the extent which this export-led growth has been managed by interventionist trade and related policies designed to protect infant industries in their early stages and to support selective export-oriented industries (various versions of so-called strategic trade theory). At the very least, it is true that most of these countries have pursued somewhat idiosyncratic paths to integration with the global economy.[12]

---

[11]   Williamson, *supra* note 10.
[12]   See Dani Rodrik, "How to Save Globalization from its Cheerleaders,"

B. Non-Reciprocal Market Access

As to the second limb of SDT – non-reciprocal trade preferences – much recent research suggests that these preferences have not proved as valuable to developing countries as they had hoped. First, the benefits of the preferences seem to be concentrated on the more advanced developing countries that needed them least. For example, a 1987 study found that four beneficiaries – Brazil, Hong Kong, Korea, and Taiwan – derived more than 50 per cent of all GSP benefits.[13] Second, GSP market access preferences have tended to become less valuable as margins of preference have been eroded through successive negotiating rounds which reduced MFN tariff levels. Third, preferences are also not durable, since they have often been tied to the level of a country's economic development; countries that are successful in increasing per capita incomes are often graduated out of the programs. Fourth, donor countries often reserve the right to withdraw preferences if imports became too competitive with domestic products. Fifth, many import-sensitive products of major export interest to developing countries have been excluded from GSP schemes. Sixth, preferences have increasingly been subject to various forms of conditionality such as human and labour rights and environmental standards, and ideological or geo-political factors (such as countries' perceived efforts to combat terrorism). Seventh, complex rules of origin also have often diluted the value of GSP preferences, preventing developing countries from producing goods most efficiently. Eighth, preferences cause trade diversion from non-preference recipient developing countries to the preference recipients. Thus, while preferences may benefit some developing countries in the short term, they are unlikely to benefit developing countries overall and they create inducements to distort comparative advantage, which puts the preference recipients at risk

---

Footnote 12 (*cont.*)
(September 2007) Working Paper 07–038, Kennedy School of Government, Harvard University; see more generally, Rodrik, *One Economy, Many Recipes: Globalization, Institutions and Economic Growth* (Princeton: Princeton University Press, 2007); Rodrik, *The Globalization Paradox* (New York: W.W. Norton & Co., 2011).

[13] Guy Karsenty and Samuel Laird, "The Generalized System of Preferences: A Quantitative Assessment of the Direct Trade Effects and of Policy Options," (Geneva, 1987) UNCTAD Discussion Paper #18.

in the long term if and when preferences are withdrawn.[14] Finally, and most importantly, because these preferences are non-reciprocal, developing countries have forsaken significant bargaining leverage in negotiations with developed countries – without a quid, there is often a very meager quo. This is simply to acknowledge the *réal politique* of trade negotiations – one has to give in order to get.

Despite these reservations about the past and prospective efficacy of SDT, some prominent and respected commentators continue to defend its continuing vitality and indeed argue for its strengthening and expansion. For example, Nobel laureate Joseph Stiglitz in two recent books[15] argues that the empirical evidence demonstrating the economic benefits of a liberal trading regime for most developing countries is much more ambiguous than conventional thinking acknowledges, pointing to the gradualist and sometimes strategic approach to trade liberalization adopted by most of the high-growth East Asian economies, the relative failure of the so-called Washington consensus to stimulate high and sustainable growth in much of Latin America, and the devastating short-run economic consequences of "shock therapy" in Russia. He argues that even if in the long run an open trading regime is to the benefit of developing countries, the absence of most of the adjustment cushions that exist in developed countries means that many developing countries face relatively more severe adjustment costs from trade liberalization. From these premises, he argues for a radically expanded form of SDT, where countries would be divided into various per capita income tranches and countries in higher income tranches would be required to liberalize all trade with countries in lower income tranches and among themselves, while countries in lower income tranches would only be required to liberalize trade with countries in even lower income tranches and among themselves but not with

---

[14] Gene M. Grossman and Alan O. Sykes, "A Preference for Development: The Law and Economics of GSP," (2005) 4:1 *World Trade Review* 41.

[15] Joseph E. Stiglitz and Andrew Charlton, *Fair Trade for All: How Trade Can Promote Development* (Oxford: Oxford University Press, 2005) and Joseph E. Stiglitz, *Making Globalization Work* (New York: W.W. Norton & Co., 2006), Chapter 3 (Making Trade Fair). For a more radical recent critique of conventional economic rationales for free trade, see Roberto M. Unger, *Free Trade Reimagined* (Princeton: Princeton University Press, 2007).

respect to trade with countries in higher income tranches. Proposals such as this, which have been vigorously endorsed by prominent international NGOs such as Oxfam, have significantly widened the fault-line between developing and developed countries in the multilateral trading system, and hence it is difficult not to be pessimistic about the prospects of finding any consensus or middle ground in the current Doha Round of multilateral trade negotiations.

C. Preferential Trading Agreements

As discussed in a previous chapter, regional and bilateral trading agreements, pursued between or among developed and developing countries, and between or among developing countries themselves, have proliferated in recent years. Since the failure of the Cancun WTO Ministerial in September 2003, for example, the U.S. has announced that it will aggressively pursue bilateral trading agreements with friendly developing countries, and indeed it has done so. As to whether this strategy provides an effective response for developing countries to the fault-lines between developing and developed countries in the multilateral system noted above, there are also reasons for pessimism. Negotiations between large developed countries and small, poor developing countries on a bilateral basis entail much greater inequalities of bargaining power and sophistication than developing countries encounter in the multilateral system, at least if they strategically negotiate as blocks or informal coalitions, exploiting the consensus decision principle that governs the multilateral system. Indeed, they are likely to end up assuming so-called WTO-plus commitments in areas such as intellectual property and investment. In turn, regional trade agreements between or among developing countries cannot, for the most part, ensure greater access to their most valuable potential export markets in developed countries.

17. Future challenges for the world trading system

Drawing together a number of the issues that have been discussed in earlier chapters in this book, several themes emerge that pose major challenges to the future of the world trading system.

1. Governance of the World Trade Organization

While the one-country one-vote and consensus principles have served the World Trading System well for much of its history, principles that worked well when the GATT/WTO system had a relatively small number of members do not work nearly as well today with a WTO membership of 153 countries in widely varying stages of economic, social, and political development, as reflected in the gridlock in the current Doha Round of multilateral trade negotiations. If the multilateral system is to be reinvigorated, the appropriate institutional analogy is not the General Assembly of the United Nations, which is largely an ineffectual talk shop, but rather the European Union where over the past 20 years substantial decision-making authority has been vested in the European Commission, whose decisions in a wide range of matters is subject to a weighted special majority vote by member countries. By analogy to the European Union, and perhaps to the recent emergence of the G20 as an important international deliberative forum in global financial matters, it seems imperative that the WTO move to some form of delegated decision-making by a broadly representative executive body charged with formulating issues for negotiation and managing initial negotiations, with recommendations subject to a trade-weighted special majority vote of all member countries. While recurring and unresolved difficulties in the way of reforming the Security Council of the U.N. suggest the difficulties that lie ahead in restructuring the WTO's decision-making organs and processes, it is likely to become increasingly marginalized in international trade matters without an ability to move in a more decisive and timely fashion on current trade issues.

2. Multilateralism versus Bilateralism

The proliferation of preferential trade agreements (PTAs) while in part, no doubt, reflecting paralysis within the multilateral system also, in turn, undermines the centrality and vitality of the latter. Revisiting the rules that should govern the creation of PTAs and, more importantly, rendering these rules effectively justiciable and enforceable are important challenges if the world trading system is not to dissolve into an ever-increasing number of discriminatory trading arrangements.

3. Developing Countries in the World Trading System

While special and differential treatment for developing countries in the GATT/WTO system has long been a feature of this system, it is far from clear that this special treatment has served many developing countries well, and tends, for the most part, to treat all developing countries – from the least developed to the large and rapidly growing – in much the same way. Compelling arguments can be made for unqualified dispensations to least-developed countries, both with respect to non-reciprocal access for their exports to other countries' markets and for very broad policy flexibility on the import side. However, with respect to other developing countries, their long-term interests are likely to be better served by fuller integration into the GATT/WTO system with relatively few dispensations on either the export or import sides, beyond the case for recognizing special *ex ante* or *ex post* safeguard regimes for highly vulnerable, subsistence agricultural sectors.

4. Trade and Cognate Areas of International Law

The increasing interface between international trade policy and a variety of cognate areas of international law, such as environmental law, labour law, and human rights law, suggests continuing to cabin international trade law as a self-contained body of international law is likely to compromise its credibility and legitimacy with a wide variety of constituencies in the future, and calls for more efforts than have hitherto occurred both at the dispute settlement and negotiating level to integrate international trade law more fully into the general corpus of public international law.

5. Contingent Protection Regimes

Antidumping duties are promiscuously applied by many countries without any coherent economic or other policy rationale, while the safeguard regime (as interpreted by the Appellate Body) is almost impossible to comply with, despite having a more coherent rationale. A major rebalancing of these two regimes is required.

6. Trade and Agriculture

In breaking the impasse in negotiations over liberalizing international trade in agriculture products, high priority should be assigned to the complete elimination of export subsidies and major liberalization of tariffs and tariff rate quotas with few dispensations except for developing countries with vulnerable traditional subsistence agricultural sectors. Conversely, fewer constraints should be imposed on domestic subsidies once a higher proportion of the costs of these are internalized to the countries providing them (precipitating higher internal levels of political accountability for these expenditures).

7. Trade Policy and Exchange Rates

While the rules of international trade law have a fair degree of stability and predictability to them, this stability and predictability is increasingly threatened by misvalued currencies and highly volatile exchange rates (and the risk of currency wars) that impact substantially on trade flows and opportunities. Better management and coordination of exchange rates, through bodies such as the G20 or the IMF, has emerged, in the wake of the recent global financial crisis, as an important complement to an open global trading system, but this challenge is only beginning to be addressed seriously.

8. Trade Policy and Foreign Direct Investment

International trade and foreign direct investment are in important respects both complements to and substitutes for each other and require some over-arching multilateral framework for their regulation. This is largely non-existent in the case of foreign direct investment, which (rather like the proliferation of PTAs) is increasingly governed by a proliferation of bilateral investment treaties (BITs) containing divergent substantive provisions and forms of dispute settlement. A balanced multilateral agreement on foreign direct investment reflecting the interests and concerns of both capital-exporting and capital-importing countries and developed and developing countries would be an important complement to the GATT/WTO system, which at present largely regulates only international trade in goods and services, and has only peripheral relevance to international movements of foreign direct investment.

Index